West Af

Other titles in the series

West African Nature Handbooks

West African Insects

John Boorman

Longman

Longman Group UK Limited
Longman House,
Burnt Mill, Harlow, Essex, UK.

First published 1981
Second impression 1991

ISBN 0 582 60626 8

Produced by Longman Group (FE) Ltd
Printed in Hong Kong

Contents

Preface

Nobody who lives in West Africa can fail to notice the abundant insect life which shares his habitat. Perhaps it would be better put the other way round, with man sharing his environment with the insects, for these creatures far and away outnumber the human population. West Africa is a paradise for the entomologist who, with a little diligent searching, can find representatives of all but one of the insect orders known to science. No one has made a complete inventory – and possibly never will – but there are certainly tens of thousands, maybe hundreds of thousands of species which occur in this part of the world.

For this reason alone it is obviously impossible to deal fully with all the West African insects in a volume the size of the present one. The butterflies and moths have been dealt with in another book of this series, and are only briefly mentioned here. For the rest, I have tried to give a general account of each of the known groups, selecting for special mention any which are commonly encountered, are particularly interesting, or are particularly important to man.

In selecting these I am well aware that I have omitted many insects which have a good claim to be included, and have given what may seem to be undue emphasis to others. However I hope that this short account will encourage those who read it to carry on from where I leave off, and I hope that it will engender a lasting interest in this fascinating group of creatures. After all, what more could the author of a book on insects wish than that his readers should be 'bitten' by the entomological 'bug'?

I should like to express my thanks here to all of my colleagues who have helped in preparing this book; to Dr A. Youdeowei for his helpful comments and suggestions and particularly to Mr K. Harris for his suggestions and critical appraisal of the manuscript.

Acknowledgements

The publishers are grateful to
the following for permission to
reproduce the colour plates:
John Boorman for Plates 1, 6, 21
and the front and back cover
photos; ICI Plant Protection
Division for Plates 15 and 16;
Natural Science Photos for
Plates 2, 3, 4, 5, 7, 8, 9, 10, 11,
12, 13, 14, 17, 18, 19, 20, 22,
23, 24, 25, 26, 27, 28, 29, 30,
31, 32 and 33.

The illustrations were drawn by
Richard Bonson.

About Insects

In order to understand insects and their way of life, we must first take a brief look at what insects are, and what their structure is. Insects belong to the section or phylum of the animal kingdom known as the Arthropoda; that is, they have a segmented body and a hard external shell or exoskeleton. They are members of the class Insecta and are closely related to other arthropods such as the Arachnida (ticks, mites, scorpions, spiders etc.), the Crustacea (crabs, lobsters, water-fleas, wood-lice etc.) and the Myriapoda (millipedes and centipedes). They are probably more closely related to the millipedes and centipedes than to other arthropods. They are often confused with spiders, ticks and mites but these have four pairs of legs instead of three pairs (although the early stages of ticks and mites have three pairs of legs).

The hard exoskeleton of insects is made mainly of a toughened protein material, which may be strengthened by a polysaccharide called chitin. The body is divided into three main sections, the head, the thorax and the abdomen, and they usually have three pairs of legs and two pairs of wings. There are, however, many variations on the basic theme and the main sections of the body are not always easy to make out. For instance, the larvae of blow-flies (maggots) have no well-defined head or thorax. Some insects have become adapted to particular ways of life and may have lost their wings or legs during the course of evolution. Fleas and lice, for instance, have become adapted to a parasitic way of life and have lost their wings. The structure of individual species may have become modified to suit particular habits. Mosquitoes and bugs, for instance, have mouthparts which are adapted for piercing animal and plant tissues and sucking blood or sap.

The head bears a pair of antennae, the mouthparts and the eyes. The antennae are sensory in function, being a sort of combined organ of taste and smell. They are extremely sensitive. In many if not most insects the female produces chemical substances called pheromones; these are attractive to the males and by following up these 'scent' trails borne on the wind the males are able to locate members of the opposite sex. In some moths the males are able to detect females of the same species over distances of several miles, and it has been shown that insects can react to as little as a single molecule of pheromone.

The mouthparts may be modified according to the feeding habits. In some insects, for example cockroaches, which feed on a wide variety of animal and vegetable matter, they are of a basic chewing type with a large pair of jaw-like mandibles. In others such as the bugs they are modified into a complex tubular structure with which the insect pierces and sucks the tissues of plants. Some insects, for example mayflies, do not feed at all and in these the mouthparts are small and simple.

The eyes are of two types. The compound eyes are large structures on each side of the head, and consist of many separate units. Each of these units has a separate lens and is capable of forming an image, although not a very clear one, and the insect is unable to focus on a particular object. The entire visual pattern is made up of a mosaic of images from each of the separate units, and movement is more readily detected than fine detail. Most insects are able to appreciate colours, although in general they are more sensitive to the shorter wavelengths (violet and blue) than to the red end of the spectrum. The simple eyes, or ocelli, are very small, two or three in number and are found on the head between and just behind the compound eyes. Their exact function is unclear but they seem to act simply as light-detecting organs rather than forming an image of the insect's surroundings.

The thorax is basically a three-segmented box which supports the wings and legs. The first segment, the prothorax, bears a pair of legs; the second, the mesothorax, and the third, the metathorax, both normally bear a pair of legs and a pair of wings. Usually these three segments are fused together and are difficult to make out but in some insects (for instance, the mantids) the prothorax is separate and mobile while in the more primitive insect, for instance the Collembola, all three segments are separate.

The legs are jointed and have

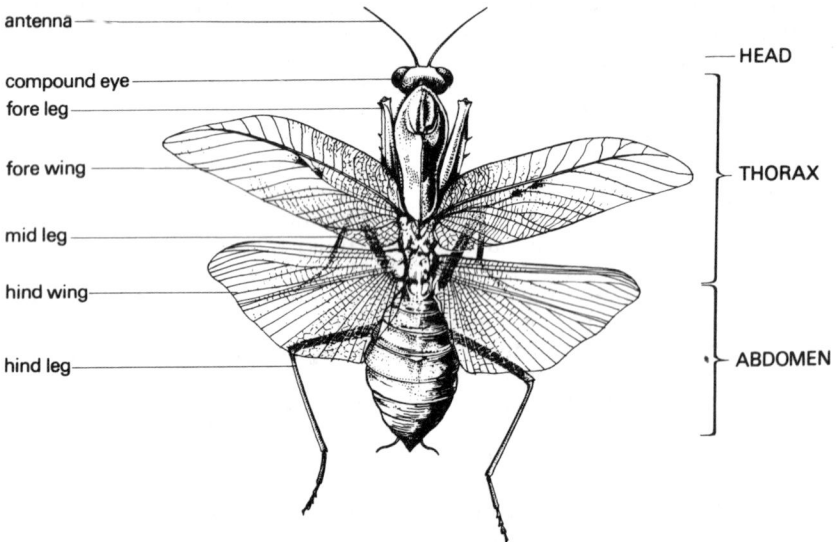

Fig 1   Mantis, showing the parts of the body

2

five main sections. These are respectively the coxa (the most basal section), the trochanter, the femur, the tibia and the tarsus; the tarsus itself usually has several separate joints. The basic pattern of the legs may be modified or adapted to serve different functions. In mole-crickets, for example, the fore-legs are flattened and strengthened to form efficient spade-like organs for digging and in fleas the hind-legs are very powerful and modified for leaping. The wings are delicate membranous structures which are strengthened by a system of fine tubes or veins (although blood does not circulate through them as in the veins of animals). The patterns made by these veins are characteristic for the different types of insects and are of great importance in the identification of groups or species. The wing may be transparent or covered with hairs or scales, and the wing membrane may be ornamented with coloured patterns.

The abdomen is segmented and does not bear any appendages, except in the more primitive orders. At the hind end there are the external genitalia and there may be two or more jointed bristle-like structures or cerci.

In the above account I have said nothing of the internal structure of insects as this is such a vast and complex subject that I suggest recourse to one of the entomological textbooks for details. Mention should be made, however, of the way in which insects breathe. They do not have lungs or a well-developed circulatory system to distribute oxygen to the tissues, as we do. Instead there are small openings, usually on each side of the thorax and abdomen, which lead into a system of branching tubes or tracheae. These in turn divide into finer tubes which take the oxygen of the air direct to the tissues. The circulation of air is assisted by pumping movements of the body. It is the efficiency (or perhaps one should say the lack of efficiency) of this system which limits the size of insects and is the reason that no insect is bulkier than about 6 cm across (although parts of some insects may be much longer). In some insects diffusion of oxygen may take place across the cuticle, particularly in aquatic insects.

Life-cycle

During their lifetime, insects undergo development through a succession of separate stages; that is, they undergo metamorphosis. This development is both external and internal, and they do not become sexually mature until the last stage. At each successive stage the insect moults, shedding its skin completely, and it is at this point that most increase in size occurs. When the insect has become adult, it ceases to grow (but there are exceptions, for instance queen termites which increase greatly in size). In the first four insect orders, that is from the Thysanura to the Collembola, there is almost no visible metamorphosis, the insects apparently simply becoming larger at each moult. The rest of the insect orders are divided into two main groups based on the type of metamorphosis.

In the first group, the Exopterygota or Hemimetabola, metamorphosis is gradual and the wings develop externally. A nymph emerges from the egg and this nymph may resemble the adult save that it is smaller, does not have wings and is not sexually mature. As the nymph grows it moults several times and wing buds appear which grow bigger at each moult. At the last moult the adult insect is revealed. This type of metamorphosis, where there is no separate pupal stage, occurs in the orders from the Ephemeroptera to the Thysanoptera, and is sometimes termed 'incomplete metamorphosis'.

In the Endopterygota or Holometabola, which have the other type of life-cycle, or 'complete metamorphosis', a larva emerges from the egg which differs from the adult both in appearance and habits. After several moults the larva enters a resting stage during which it does not feed but development of the adult takes place internally. This is the pupal stage and this type of metamorphosis is found in all the orders from the Neuroptera to the Strepsiptera.

As will become apparent from the accounts of the various insect orders which follow, there are many variations on these two basic themes. The nymphs of dragonflies and mayflies do not resemble the adults at all, and have quite different habits. Some insects, for instance some species of cockroaches and tsetse flies, are viviparous and give birth to living nymphs or larvae instead of laying eggs. In a few insects parthenogenesis occurs, that is, unfertilised females may lay viable eggs. In these cases (as in some stick-insects) the males may occur only very rarely or there may be separate generations when males do not occur (as in aphids).

Classification

Insects are divided by entomologists into a number of separate sections or orders, the members of which have certain features in common. These orders each have a scientific name and, in some cases, a common name. Thus the Isoptera are termites and the Hemiptera are bugs. However, whereas the scientific names are invariable and the same the whole world over, the common names may vary and may even be misleading. An alternative name for termite is 'white ant', but termites have no connection with ants. For this reason it is better to learn and use the scientific names. It is no more difficult in the long run and will make reference to other entomological literature considerably easier. Each insect order is made up of a number of sub-divisions or families. These are made up of different genera and these in turn comprise a number of species. Each insect species has a scientific name of two parts, a generic name which comes first and is written with a capital letter, and a specific name. For instance the scientific name for the yellow fever mosquito is *Aedes aegypti*. However it has recently become recognised that there may be differences below that of the species, which may be vitally important. A good example of this is *Simulium damnosum*, the black-fly which is responsible for the transmission of river blindness in West Africa. Studies on the chromosomes of populations of this fly have shown that more than twenty genetically different forms of the fly exist, although externally they are almost indistinguishable. The important thing is that these genetically different forms may have different habits, so that a control measure used against one form may be quite ineffective when applied against another. This type of study is one of the many exciting and important fields of present-day entomological research.

Why study insects?

Why do we bother to study insects at all? There are several answers to this. For a start, they are creatures of considerable beauty and intrinsic general interest. They probably far outnumber any other living animal. They have an astonishing diversity of size and form; the smallest measure only about 1 mm or less and the largest perhaps 30 cm long. They have colonised land, air and water, although there are very few insects which actually live in the sea. Some insects can withstand high temperatures or resist desiccation for long periods and there are even insects whose larvae live in pools of crude oil. They are masters of the air, and one has only to watch a dragonfly in flight over a pond to appreciate this.

Another reason for studying them is that they present many interesting features of behaviour and are important in many ecosystems. Many insects migrate over long distances, and the study of such movements may help to predict outbreaks of insect pests. Insects present many degrees of social organisation, from those which live in small groups of a few individuals to those which live in colonies of many thousands and have a complex social structure. The behaviour of insects, for instance the ways in which some solitary wasps find and capture the insects on which their larvae feed, is a study in itself. There may be a delicate natural balance between insects and other creatures, or between different species of insects, as for example the delicate balance between pests and predators on cocoa and the influence of such a balance on the spread of disease. The relation between insects and their environment is a delicate one. Changing land usage is a major factor in changing insect populations and by clearing natural forests, for example, we are destroying for ever insect populations before we even begin to understand them.

Most importantly, perhaps, insects affect the lives of all of us, either directly or indirectly. Some are directly harmful to us. They may occur in such numbers as to create a nuisance, or have an unpleasant smell as in the case of some stink-bugs. They may bite or sting, as in the case of some ants. Some insects transmit diseases to livestock and other animals, and the role of insects in the transmission of disease to man will be well known to readers. Malaria, yellow fever, filariasis, river blindness and sleeping sickness are a constant threat and immense sums are spent annually on attempts to control the vectors of these diseases. There are considerable annual losses of cattle and other livestock due to the activities of insects. Insects destroy our crops and reduce yields, and also destroy crop produce, for instance stored grain. It has been estimated that there are in Africa about 450 different insect pests of cotton, 150 of maize and other cereals and over 100 of citrus and sugar cane.

Not all insects are harmful, of course. There is a vast army of insect scavengers constantly at work clearing away animal dung and corpses, without which the world would be a considerably less pleasant place. Insects play a major role in the pollination of plants, and without the insects there would be many fewer crops. Cocoa, for instance, is pollinated by small flies and without these there would be no cocoa-producing industry. The vast majority of insects are neither directly harmful nor beneficial, but are nevertheless of vital importance in the general balance of nature.

Insect control

How do we control insects which are harmful to us? Many methods are available, but for any to be successful we must have a good knowledge of the biology of the insect in question. In some cases populations may be reduced by indirect methods such as practising crop rotation, or by breeding varieties of plants which are resistant to particular diseases. Improved hygiene may reduce populations of pests such as cockroaches or bed-bugs. A good example of indirect control is that of the 'bush' fly in Australia. These are a considerable pest in some areas. The flies breed in animal dung which would normally be removed and buried by dung beetles. Unfortunately there are no native dung beetles in Australia, and large sums have been spent in attempts to introduce dung beetles which would get rid of the dung and in turn reduce the fly problem.

Chemical methods may also be used to control pests but these are often expensive and to be effective must be employed on a large scale, as for instance against locusts, mosquitoes or cocoa capsid bugs. These chemical insecticides may be either a poison bait, which is taken in during feeding, or a chemical which is sprayed on surfaces that the insect rests on or comes into contact with, and then is absorbed through the skin of the insect. Poison baits may be used against such pests as cockroaches and ants. Since these feed on a wide variety of foods the poison can be mixed with bran or cake and scattered where the insects will find it. Care must always be taken that such poisoned bait cannot be eaten by domestic pets or small children. Insecticide sprays may be effective for only a few days or for several months, depending upon the chemical used and the surface on which it is applied. Some of the most effective of the insecticides have now been recognised to be dangerous to humans and animals. They are such persistent substances that traces of poison build up in animals and birds which feed on insects and these traces are then passed on to humans. Whenever insecticides are used they should be treated for what they are, that is, poisons, and they should only be used as recommended by the manufac- turers. In some special cases, particularly for control of pests of stored products, fumigation is used. The chemicals used in these cases are very dangerous if used improperly, and this type of control should be left strictly to the professionals.

The widespread use of chemicals for control is always best avoided if possible, and much research has been devoted to methods of 'biological control'. As will be seen later, many insects live as parasites on other insects at some stage of their life-cycle. If a suitable parasite can be found for a pest species, and then introduced into the area where the pest is a problem, dramatic control may sometimes be obtained. However, there are many snags to this attractive idea and much research must be carried out on the biology of both the host and the parasite. One must be careful that the parasite itself will not become a pest, nor will destroy other insects which may be beneficial. All of this work takes a long time, and time must also be allowed for populations of the parasite to become established. Where practicable, however, this method is very effective and usually permanent, as populations of parasite and host eventually achieve a natural balance.

Another biological method often used on pest species, particularly moths, uses the pheromones produced by the female insect. This substance is isolated from the insect and then synthesised in the laboratory. If one is lucky (the process is not as easy as it sounds) the synthetic substance will be attractive to males of the same species, and may be used in traps to capture large numbers of males and thus reduce the population. This method has the great advantage that the pheromones are often highly species-specific, so that only insects of the pest species are trapped and destroyed.

Insects themselves often fall victim to infections with viruses and bacteria, and use of this has been made to control pests. A virus or bacterium which is fatal to a particular pest is grown in large amounts in the laboratory, and then sprayed where the pest species occurs. This results in an epidemic of disease which decimates the population. This method has worked well in some cases but must be used with great caution in case the disease agent used infects creatures other than insects. Other types of insect parasite, such as fungi or nematode worms, may also be used in this way and show promise as possible control organisms.

Much research is going on with two other biological control methods, and which shows great promise. One is to introduce large numbers of sterile male insects into the pest population. The insects are reared in the laboratory and are sterilised by radiation. When these are released into the wild they mate with wild females which then lay infertile eggs. This technique can only be used with success on insects which mate only once during their life and where the insects can be reared in large enough numbers to ensure a large excess of sterile over wild males. It has been used with great success in America for control of the screw-worm fly, and shows considerable promise in Africa for tsetse control; trials have already been carried out in West Africa. The other method is 'genetic control', whereby insects having some disadvantageous (to them) factor are introduced into the wild population. This may be some lethal factor which reduces survival, or it may be a factor that confers resistance in a vector to a particular parasite. In this way the pest species is put at a disadvantage or is rendered less efficient as a disease vector. However a great deal of careful research must be carried out

before such methods are used and although it shows great promise it has not yet been used in Africa.

Collecting insects

What if one wishes to collect insects, or to preserve a choice specimen for further study? In general, the more delicate or tiny insects are best preserved in a fluid such as 70% alcohol or 5–10% formalin, or mounted on microscope slides as permanent mounts. Larger, more robust insects such as beetles or bugs can be dried after their wings and legs have been spread out and if stored in boxes away from damp with a little preservative will keep for many years. Suitable preservatives are naphthalene, paradichlorobenzene (both are sold in chemists as moth repellents for clothes) or beechwood creosote (not the sort used for preserving timber) which may be purchased from a chemist.

Insects may be caught in bottles and tubes, or in a net. Many insects are attracted to bright lights at night and collecting at night is an excellent way to start a study of them.

Many entomological textbooks give details of collecting, preserving and rearing insects. Two of the most useful are 'Introduction to Insect Study in Africa' by E.C.G. Pinhey and 'A Laboratory Manual of Entomology' by A. Youdeowei which not only gives an excellent account of methods for collecting, preserving and identifying African insects but also deals with African examples of the various orders and details simple experiments with insects.

The apparatus needed for collecting insects is fairly simple and with a little ingenuity can often be home-made. Once collected, it is important that they should have full data as to the date and locality of collection and any other relevant information such as the name of the captor. This data should be written on a label and attached to the pin of the specimen or put in the jar or tube with the specimen.

Identifying insects

Identification of a particular insect species is often a problem for the amateur collector (and frequently for the professional entomologist!). The best advice to anyone contemplating studying insects is to contact someone in the Zoology department of your nearest University. You will find them only too pleased to assist, or they will put you in contact with someone who can help, and you may find that there is a reference collection of insects with which you can compare your captures. There are research centres in many of the major West African cities which will help if asked and they will be able to tell you if there is any local society which can help you. The Nigerian Field Society has branches in most large towns in Nigeria and in many other West African countries; through such a society you will meet others with similar interests. The Entomological Society of Nigeria, founded in 1965 and originally based at Ibadan University has widespread activities and produces a range of excellent publications. Above all, do not be afraid to ask for advice. Entomologists are a friendly bunch of people who are always pleased to find a fellow enthusiast! The other source of information is books. There are many excellent books on insects, but few which deal specifically with West Africa. I have given a selection of those which are most readily available and which the reader may find of most use, in the reference section at the end of this book.

Thysanura and Collembola
(Bristletails and Springtails)

These two orders together with the Diplura and Protura form the sub-class Apterygota, the insects without wings. They are all small insects, and as such often escape notice. They have many primitive features, for example some Collembola and Diplura lack a tracheal system. Relatively little is known of the biology of most of these insects, especially in West Africa. Some 2,500 species are known but doubtless many more remain to be discovered, especially in the tropics.

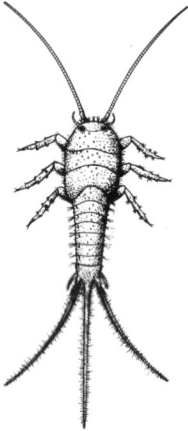

Fig 2   Bristletail (Thysanura)

The Thysanura or bristletails (Fig 2) are among the most primitive of all insects. They are found mostly in soil and amongst decaying vegetation although some are found living in the nests of ants and termites, where they presumably act as scavengers. Most of them are white or brown in colour and some have a covering of silvery scales which gives them a metallic appearance. They may be recognised by the three 'tails' at the end of the abdomen. Bristletails are some-times found in houses among books, papers, on shelves or in cupboards. One type popularly known as a 'silverfish' is found in larders, where it lives by scavenging fragments of food. They are seldom found in such numbers as to cause a nuisance, and do no harm.

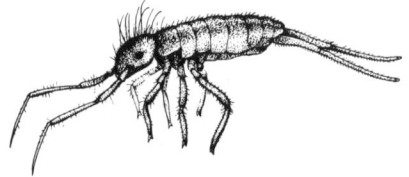

Fig 3   Springtail (Collembola)

The largest (in terms of numbers) and most well known of these four orders is the Collembola (Fig 3), otherwise known as 'springtails'. They are all small insects, rarely more than 4—5 mm long, and are found in damp places, usually in associa-tion with decaying organic matter. Many are found in soil or in leaf litter. Some species are found in the nests of ants and termites, others are found on the surface of puddles or ponds. Most of them are dark brown or black in colour, but some have attractive patterns of yellow and white. They are most easily recognised by their habit of jumping into the air. They do this by using a forked organ called the 'furcula' which is to be found at the end of the abdomen, and is normally held folded forwards and underneath the body. When the insect jumps the furcula is released and strikes the ground forcibly, pushing the insect up into the air. Usually springtails are quite harmless, but some species can damage seedling plants if present in large numbers. The damage is caused by large numbers of insects chewing at the soft growing parts of the plants. They are sometimes found in vast hordes in the filter beds of sewage works where they perform a valuable service by preventing the gravel from clogging. Occasionally, large aggregations of adults and immature forms have been noted. This type of behaviour has been recorded in Nigeria, where they were described as large blackish patches on forest roads and which consisted of myriads of individuals. By the next day they had disappeared, but whether they were migrating or just dispersing from a breeding site is not known.

The life-histories of all four orders seem to be similar in that eggs are laid in damp places and hatch into minute nymphs which look very like the adults. They undergo several moults before they become mature, and the life-cycle may take a few weeks or several months.

Ephemeroptera *(Mayflies)*

The common name of this order refers to the habit of the adults of emerging mostly in the spring in temperate climates and the scientific name refers to the brief ephemeral life of the adult. The life-cycle is of the 'incomplete' type, and is unique among insects in that a 'sub-imago' stage occurs.

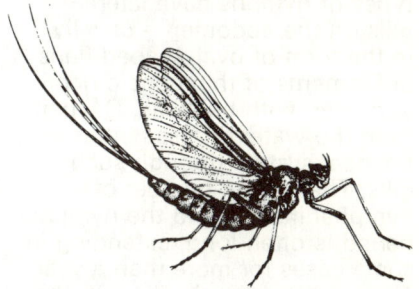

Fig 4   Adult mayfly (Ephemeroptera) — the wings are held above the body when at rest

Adult mayflies (Fig 4) are small to moderate-sized insects, most having a wing span of less than 4 cm. They have two pairs of wings, of which the front pair is the larger. The body has two or three long 'tails', which form a distinctive feature of the group. The mouthparts are rudimentary, and most species do not feed as adults. They are usually very short-lived, and in some cases the adult stage lasts only a few hours; at the most it is only a few days. They are most often found near water. At certain times of · the year mass emergences may occur. The adults may then be seen flying up and down in swarms over the surface of ponds and rivers, in the late afternoon or early evening. They are often attracted to lights at night.

The life-cycle starts with the eggs, which are laid in the water or on aquatic plants. The nymphs which hatch are fully aquatic and live beneath the surface on water plants or among rocks, where they feed upon plants and algae, or other vegetable debris. Most types of nymphs have lateral gills on the abdomen — usually in the form of oval-shaped flaps or filaments of thin cuticle richly endowed with tracheae. Oxygen from the water diffuses into the tracheal system through such gills. There are a number of nymphal instars, and the nymphal period is often long, extending in some cases for more than a year. This contrasts markedly with the brief adult life.

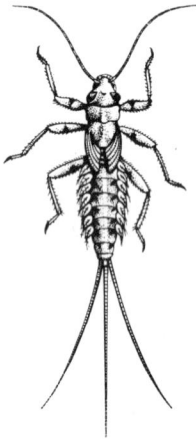

Fig 5   Mayfly nymph

When the nymph (Fig 5) is fully grown it climbs out of the water and the cuticle splits to reveal a 'sub-imago'. This is very like the adult, having fully developed wings and being capable of flight; but it is rather more dull-coloured than the true adult and its wings are translucent rather than transparent. After a short period, which may be only an hour or two, the sub-imago sheds its skin completely, even to the extent of the thin membrane covering the wings. The adult is then revealed in its full colouring; some species are brownish but others are brightly coloured, with reds and yellows predominating.

Both the adults and nymphs of mayflies form an important part of the aquatic food chain, and are an important item of diet for fish. They are not normally of any economic significance to man, except in the rare cases when they occur in such vast numbers as to become a nuisance. The presence of mayfly nymphs is a useful indication of a low degree of pollution of the water in which they occur because they are absent in even moderately polluted streams and ponds.

Odonata *(Dragonflies)*

In most parts of West Africa, and especially around water, one cannot help but notice the dragonflies — large, brightly coloured insects with long, transparent wings and remarkable powers of flight (Plate 1). The wings have a very elaborate network of fine veins, and the front wings closely resemble the hind pair. The adults are very strong fliers — they can hover and even fly backwards. They feed on other insects which they capture on the wing. As might be expected of insects with this habit, they have large, well-developed compound eyes, and the head is very mobile, being joined to the thorax by a thin neck. Dragonflies are among the oldest insects of which we have fossil records and dragonflies were abundant long before mammals evolved. Some of them were giants, and fossils found in carboniferous deposits measure as much as 60 cm across the wings. Today, the order contains two main sections, the sub-order *Zygoptera* or damselflies (Plate 2), which are slender-bodied insects with a relatively slow fluttering flight, and the sub-order *Anisoptera* or dragonflies, robustly-built swift-flying insects. There are probably about 300 West African species; the largest measures about 13 cm and the smallest about 2 cm across the wings. They have an incomplete type of metamorphosis, and like mayflies and stoneflies the nymphs are quite unlike the adults.

The eggs are laid either singly or in batches in water, where they sink to the bottom, or in slits made by the females in the stems or leaves of water plants. Some types of eggs have elaborate patterns on the shell and long filaments, which serve to entangle the eggs in vegetation or debris and prevent them from being washed away in fast-flowing water. The nymphal stage is passed in water, usually fresh although there are some species which breed in brackish water. Some live in the temporary collections of water found in rock-pools and these have a very rapid life-cycle, since the nymphs cannot withstand the drying out of the habitat. Most species of this type are found in savannah areas.

The nymphs are dull brownish in colour, blending in with their surroundings, and live either in the mud at the bottom or among water plants. They are voracious predators, feeding on other water

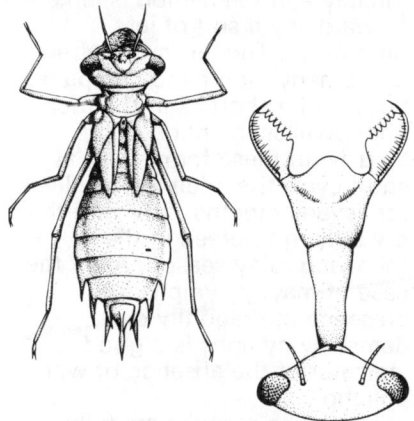

Fig 6   Dragonfly nymph (Odonata) and the head of a nymph with the mask extended

13

creatures, the larger species even preying upon tadpoles or small fish. They capture their prey by means of a pair of extensible jaw-like structures (really modified palps) on a 'mask' which is normally held folded beneath the head (Fig 6). When a potential victim comes within range the mask is shot out to grab it. The mask is then retracted and the unfortunate creature is devoured.

The nymphs breathe either by absorbing oxygen through the skin or by means of special gills. The nymphs of damselflies commonly have large terminal gills at the hind end of the abdomen. Nymphs of dragonflies normally breathe by sucking water in through the anus into the hind part of the gut which is liberally supplied with fine tracheae through which gaseous exchange takes place. They are also able to use this mechanism to move rapidly; the water which has been sucked in is expelled forcibly and the nymph is jerked forwards by a sort of jet propulsion. The life-cycle often takes many months to complete, but may be short as in the rock-pool dwellers mentioned pre-viously. In these forms with a short cycle the adult usually lives for several months, surviving the dry season to breed in the following rainy season. As in the case of mayfly nymphs, the presence of dragonfly or damselfly nymphs is a good indicator of the absence of water pollution.

When the nymphs are fully developed they climb out of the water on to a stick, stem or piece of rock. The skin dries and splits and the adult insect emerges, expands and dries its wings. Freshly emerged dragonflies and damselflies have very delicate, shiny wings and the full colours of the adult are not developed until the insect is several days old.

Most adult dragonflies are brightly coloured, these colours being due either to pigment just below the cuticle (mostly reds and yellows, and some blues and greens) or to interference colours generated in the cuticle (metallic greens and blues). Dragonflies make disappointing insects for a collection because the pigment-generated colours rapidly disappear following death. Freeze-drying can preserve some of the colours, but this process is beyond the facilities of most amateur collectors. The best way of collecting these (and indeed most insects) is by photographing them in their natural habitats.

Dragonflies are often confused with some Neuroptera (Myrmeliontidae or Ascalaphidae). The most noticeable difference is that the latter have very obvious antennae whereas in the Odonata the antennae are very tiny, bristle-like structures. Dragonflies are not known to be harmful to man and although their appearance is fearsome they do not bite or sting. There are no known pest species.

Plecoptera *(Stoneflies)*

This is a small order of insects which are found in or near fast-running streams. The adults (Fig 7) are drab brown in colour, seldom more than 3–4 cm across the wings which are clear and membraneous. They are held flat over the body when the insect is at rest, distinguishing them immediately from the mayflies. The antennae are long and filamenteous, and there are two long 'tails' at the end of the abdomen.

on small insects and other water creatures. The life-cycle may take more than a year to complete, and the nymphs moult a large number of times before they mature. They then crawl out of the water, and the adult emerges, leaving the last nymphal skin attached to a rock or twig. The adults are poor fliers and are more active at dusk than during the day. They have weak biting mouthparts and some species are said to feed on lichens and algae, but very little seems to be known of their biology. They are of no economic significance in West Africa, and do not bite or sting.

Fig 7   Adult stonefly (Plecoptera) – the wings are folded
flat over the body when at rest

The eggs are laid in batches on stones or vegetation in streams, especially those which are fast-flowing. The nymphs are found on or under stones and can be recognised by their long antennae and the two abdominal 'tails'. They look like small versions of the adult, but without wings. They breathe partly with the aid of small tufts of gills on each side of the body and they feed

Orthoptera
(Crickets, Grasshoppers and Locusts)

The grasshoppers and crickets will be familiar to most people, if only because of the sound they make, which is so much a part of the West African scene. This sound is produced either by rubbing the legs against the wings or by rubbing the wings together. This method of sound production is known as 'stridulation'. The front pair of wings is narrow and thickened; the hind pair are broad and membraneous with a network of fine veins, and are folded fan-wise when not in use. They all have mouthparts which are adapted for chewing and biting. Most live entirely on plant material but some are carnivorous and crickets tend to be omnivorous. The order is divided into several families, of which the bush-crickets, the crickets, the mole-crickets and the short-horned grasshoppers are the most familiar.

Bush-crickets (Tettigoniidae) have very long, thin slender antennae which are held either forwards or backwards over the body (Plate 3). They are usually to be found on herbage, bushes or trees, and are often green in colour. In many species the fore-wings are broad and leaf-like, some even having blotches and markings which look like leaf veins. This makes them very difficult to detect when at rest. In most species the eggs are laid in slits made in the stems of plants by the female and the life-cycle is otherwise very much like that of the short-horned grasshoppers,

which is described on page 17. The males stridulate by rubbing the wings together and they have auditory organs on the front legs.

Crickets (Gryllidae) are in general more robustly built than the grasshoppers, and have long thin antennae which are usually held forwards. The hind-legs are very well-developed and powerful, and more adapted for running than for jumping. Most species are brown in colour, but some are green. They are more usually seen at night than during the day, when they hide among vegetation, under stones or in burrows in the ground. The sound made by the males is produced by rubbing the wings together, and the auditory organs are on the front legs, as in the bush-crickets. Crickets are expert ventriloquists, and it is often impossible to tell from which direction the sound is coming. When located it is surprising how loud and penetrating a noise they can make and it is said that some species can be heard from a mile away. The eggs are usually laid singly, in the ground, although a few species lay their eggs in slits in leaves or twigs.

Mole-crickets (Gryllotalpidae: the commonest species is *Gryllotalpa africana*) are quite extraordinary creatures, as anyone who has examined one closely will know. The adults (Plate 4) are about 3–4 cm long, brown, and often attracted to lights at night. During the day they live in burrows in the ground. The front pair of legs is modified for burrowing, the distal segments being flattened, broad and turned outwards like two spades. They are like the fore-legs of a mole and by moving its legs back and forth the cricket is able to dig with great speed. If held in the hand they will quickly escape by burrowing between the fingers, unless held so tightly that they cannot move. The eggs are laid singly in chambers in the ground and the egg stage lasts two to three weeks. The nymphs undergo several moults before becoming adults and they live for about ten months, after which the adults live for three months or more. Mole-crickets can cause considerable damage to crops, for example seedling rice or oil palms, by their burrowing.

Short-horned grasshoppers and locusts (Acrididae), as their name implies, have short, stout antennae which are always held forwards. Most grasshoppers are green or brown, but some have blue or red hind-wings. This is a type of defensive colouration. When disturbed, they fly up and the coloured hind-wings make them very conspicuous. When they settle and close their wings, they are very difficult to find, since their dull fore-wings make them blend perfectly into the background. Some grasshoppers are long and thin with elongated heads. When at rest the antennae are held stiffly together and the whole insect resembles a plant stem. Other species are very short and stubby and look like large brown seeds.

The familiar 'churring' noise is made by the males, which rub the inner side of the hind-leg against a vein of the fore wing. The auditory organs are on either side of the first segment of the abdomen, not on the legs as in the crickets. The eggs are laid in sandy ground by the female, which digs a hole by stretching and contracting the abdomen. At the bottom of the hole, which may be 5—8 cm deep, she lays the eggs in a 'pod' formed of a foamy secretion which soon hardens into a tough, horny covering. When the eggs hatch, the nymphs force their way to the surface. They resemble a small version of the adult, except that the wings are represented only by short wing-buds. They feed on vegetation, and after a number of moults during which the wing-buds get progressively bigger, they become adults. Short-horned grasshoppers are found almost everywhere. Some are important as the intermediate hosts of tapeworms of poultry, others as agricultural pests because of the damage their feeding activities cause to plants.

The variegated grasshopper, *Zonocerus variegatus*, (Plates 5 and 6) is a widespread pest of a variety of crops, particularly of cassava and maize. It is a striking insect, being black, with yellow, green and red markings. The bright colour is a warning that it is distasteful to potential predators and if handled it may discharge a foul-smelling fluid from the thorax and abdomen. This grasshopper is particularly abundant during the dry season in the southern parts of Nigeria, and has been designated a National pest by the Nigerian Agricultural Advisory Council. The eggs are laid in masses in the soil at the end of the dry season and take several months to hatch.

The most notorious members of this family are the locusts. Four types are of importance in West Africa. The tree locust, *Anacridium* is occasionally reported as occurring in small swarms from the north, but these swarms are only local and are of minor importance. The red locust, *Nomadacris* occurred as large swarms in Chad in 1930, but is not usually of major importance. The desert locust, *Schistocerca gregaria*, is found in the northernmost savannah. It is not important as a pest further south than Mali and Niger, although it may occasionally extend southwards to latitude 8° north. Swarms of desert locusts often fly into West Africa on migration from North Africa but they seldom breed further south than latitude 12° north. The other type, the African migratory locust, *Locusta migratoria*, (Plate 8) is also found in the northern parts of the West African territories. In the past it has, from time to time, spread southwards in vast swarms but it is now well controlled in its outbreak areas. One of the most devastating outbreaks was one that occurred in 1928 in Niger, and continued for over ten years. It was very bad in 1929–1930, when it spread from Benin and the south-west corner of Nigeria to the whole of the north. The last swarms from this outbreak were reported in 1940.

The eggs of locusts are laid in 'pods' in sandy soil. These contain about fifty to one hundred eggs each and are laid 10–12 cm deep. Breeding takes place in the rainy season. When the nymphs hatch they force their way to the surface and attack a variety of plants, particularly cereal crops. Each locust consumes roughly its own weight of food each day. There are five instars before the nymphs become adult. The nymphs run, crawl and hop but the adults disperse by flight.

It has been found that locusts can exist in two distinct forms, one a 'solitary' phase, when they live and behave like any ordinary grasshopper, and a 'gregarious' phase. When this occurs the locusts breed in vast numbers, the small nymphs or 'hoppers' aggregate into bands and the adults collect in flying swarms, having marked migratory tendencies. Outbreaks of migratory locusts start from well-defined permanent outbreak centres, and when the combination of ecological factors is just right, the number of locusts increases and migrations start. Migrations occur mostly at the beginning or the end of the rains. The statistics are impressive as it has been estimated that locust swarms may contain as many as 1,000,000,000 individuals; that such a swarm (at 1 gram per locust) would weigh about 1,000,000 kg; and that these would consume their own weight of vegetation daily. Swarms may travel some 3,500 km in a month.

Locusts may be controlled by insecticides in the form of sprays or poison bait. Swarms may be sprayed with insecticide from the air or from ground vehicles, or vegetation may be sprayed from the air. Insecticide may be mixed with corn or bran and spread on the ground in the path of bands of hoppers. Locust control is a highly organised, technical, internationally-controlled operation, since these insects are no respecters of international boundaries. It is the constant vigilance and efforts of these organisations that keeps the locust threat in check. Two such bodies are the Organisation International contre les Criquet Migrateur Africain (OICMA), centred at Bamako in Mali, and the Organisation Commun de Lutte Anti-Acridienne et de Lutte Anti-Avian (OCLALAV), centred in Dakar in Senegal. Control in the outbreak areas is far from easy since these are scattered and mostly in inaccessible places but such measures have worked well against the African migratory and red locusts.

Phasmida *(Stick-insects and Leaf-insects)*

The stick-insects (Plate 9) are long and slender, with long thin legs and long antennae. With their green or brown colouration and their habit of remaining motionless for long periods they closely resemble a stick or twig. They are usually active at night; if disturbed by day they fall to the ground with their legs drawn up tightly to the body and feign death. When fully grown most measure about 10–12 cm long, but there are species in Asia which measure as much as 30 cm or more. Leaf-insects are flattened with leaf-like expansions of the body and legs, but they do not occur in Africa.

The eggs are laid singly and are usually dropped haphazardly on the ground. They are relatively large, have hard shells, resemble small seeds and may take several months to hatch. The small nymphs resemble the adults closely except in size and there are four or five moults before the insect matures. If a nymph loses a leg, this may be regenerated at the next moult. Some species have wings, which are often larger in the male than in the female. In some species the males are very rare and reproduction occurs by parthenogenesis. Some mantids resemble stick insects, but they may easily be distinguished by the front legs, which are long and slender in the stick-insects but adapted for catching and grasping the prey in the mantids.

Stick-insects are vegetarians, but do not usually occur in large enough numbers to be of any importance as pests. Very little is known of the biology of the West African species. They are easily kept in captivity, and make interesting insects for study.

Dermaptera and Embioptera
(Earwigs and Web-spinners)

The earwigs and web-spinners are two small orders of insects which are widely distributed. Earwigs are familiar as pests but the web-spinners are not often seen. They both present interesting features in their biology which make them worthy of study.

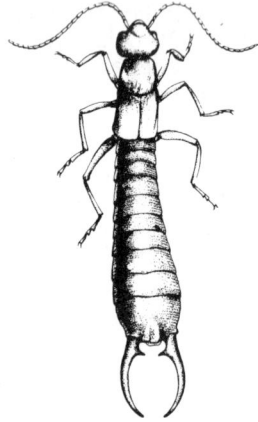

Fig 8   Earwig (Dermaptera)

Earwigs (Fig 8) are recognised by the very short, stiff wing-cases and by the pincer-like cerci at the hind end of the body. The wing-cases (modified fore-wings) hide a much-folded, very delicate and membranous pair of hind-wings. They are quite good fliers, although not often seen in flight. When they settle, the hind-wings are folded away under the wing-cases with the aid of the cerci and it is astonishing to watch the precision with which this delicate manoeuvre is accomplished.

Most species are less than 3 cm long, and are brown in colour. They are usually nocturnal, and hide away during the day under bark or stones, or among vegetation. They feed on a variety of both animal and vegetable matter. The eggs are laid in batches under bark or stones and are guarded by the female, which also guards the small nymphs when they hatch. This type of rudimentary parental care is also found in the web-spinners and in a few bugs.

A very curious member of this order, *Hemimerus*, is commonly found as a parasite on the giant rat, *Cricetomys*. These insects have no wings or eyes and are viviparous, and feed upon the skin-scales of their host. Earwigs are not as common in West Africa as in more temperate regions. There, they can occur in large numbers and can do considerable damage by biting the growing points of crops and flowers. Although the cerci look like formidable weapons, and if annoyed the earwig will flourish them threateningly, they are not capable of inflicting a bite or sting.

Web-spinners (Fig 9) are very seldom seen unless one searches for them. They are occasionally attracted to light but as they look like a small termite they are easily overlooked. They are small insects, less than 2−3 cm long. The males have two pairs of simple, narrow wings while the females are wingless. They are found mostly on the trunks of trees, in crevices in the bark or beneath the bark of decaying trees, or under stones. The abdomen bears a small pair of cerci at the hind end, but these are not pincer-like as in the earwigs. Web-spinners derive their name from their habit of constructing webs and tunnels of silk in which a group of individuals, males, females and nymphs, lives. These webs can cover much of the surface of a tree trunk and resemble spider's webs. The silk is produced by both sexes from glands on the front legs.

Like earwigs, they feed on a variety of animal and vegetable matter, and have a similar type of life-history. Again, as in the earwigs, the females of some species show a type of rudimentary parental care. These insects are quite harmless.

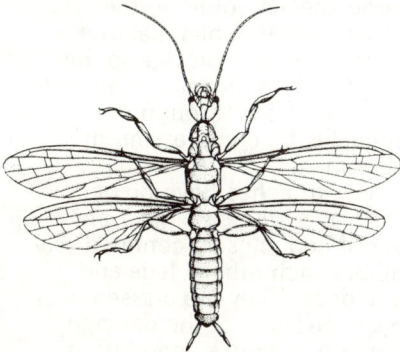

Fig 9   Adult web-spinner (Embioptera), ventral view

Dictyoptera (*Cockroaches and Mantids*)

Cockroaches and mantids have two pairs of wings with a fine, net-like pattern of veins. The front pair is rather harder and thicker than the hind-wings, which are broad and folded fan-wise over the back when not in use. Both cockroaches and mantids are good fliers and the legs of cockroaches are particularly well-adapted for running.

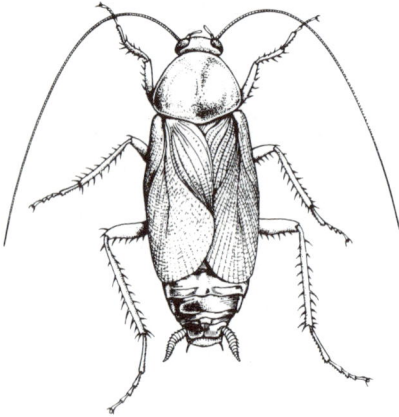

Fig 10   Adult cockroach (Dictyoptera)

Cockroaches (Fig 10) give rise to feelings of revulsion in most people. Their brown colour, their habit of scuttling away when disturbed and their objectionable smell contributes to this. The familiar American cockroach (*Periplaneta americana*) is a well known cosmopolitan pest and is a typical example of the group. The adults are brown with a rather oily appearance, about 4–5 cm long, have well developed wings and long thin antennae. The eggs are laid in a hard dark brown case, the ootheca, which measures some 5–6 mm by 3 mm. This protrudes from the end of the abdomen of the female for some days before she deposits it in some out-of-the-way place. The ootheca contains thirty to forty eggs, which hatch into small nymphs looking like wingless adults. Nymphs and adults are usually found together but there is no evidence of parental care as in the earwigs. A number of moults take place before the nymphs become adult. Cockroaches are often parasitised by small wasps called 'ensign flies', which belong to the family Evaniidae (see page 69).

There are many species of cockroach and only a very few of these are found in the domestic type of habitat. Some of the non-domestic African species are very large and indeed quite handsome insects. Some species do not lay eggs, but are viviparous, giving birth to small living nymphs. One large species found in the Malagasy Republic makes a hissing noise if picked up, by filling the tracheae with air and blowing it out through the spiracles by compressing the abdomen.

Cockroaches have powerful jaws and will eat almost anything and if kept closely confined will nibble each others' legs and antennae. They are classed as pests because of the damage they do to books and clothes and because of the way in which they contaminate premises and food with faecal material. Because of their dirty habits they have often been suspected of spreading disease, and they can harbour a variety of bacteria and viruses for a short time. There is some evidence that they may be important in this respect in such places as hotels and hospitals. They do not bite or sting and infestations are best dealt with by a combination of hygiene, insecticidal sprays and poison baits.

Mantids (the names mantid and mantis are synonymous) always give the impression of having an alert, intelligent nature since their long slender neck allows them considerable freedom to twist their head and to follow movement with their eyes. In reality though they are no more intelligent than other insects. They are easily recognised by the form of the front legs, which are modified for seizing and holding the prey. The only other insects with similar front legs are the mantispids (Neuroptera) which differ in the structure of the wings and in having shorter antennae. The common large green *Sphodromantis* is a typical member of this group of insects.

Adult mantids (Plate 10) have well-developed wings. The fore-wings are usually narrow and coloured, but the hind pair are usually colourless and broad with a fine network of veins. They fly mostly at night and are often attracted to bright lights, but whether the attraction is the light itself or other insects it is hard to say. The antennae are long and thread-like, and the head bears a pair of large prominent compound eyes and powerful jaws. It is joined to a very elongated prothorax by a narrow neck.

Mantids feed on other insects and the front legs are adapted in a remarkable fashion for seizing the prey. They are much broader and more muscular than the hind or mid-legs. The first joint, the coxa, is much longer than usual, affording extra reach and the third and fourth joints (femur and tibia) are armed with a fearsome row of interlocking spines. There is also a long spine at the end of the tibia and the mantid's unfortunate victim is held impaled between these rows of spines and eaten alive. In colour mantids are usually green or brown but some species have striking eye-like spots on the fore-wings while others may have spine-like or leaf-like projections on the head and thorax. In all they are well camouflaged to resemble the leaves and twigs among which they spend most of the day.

Mantids feed on other insects which come within reach, or the prey may be stalked slowly and deliberately over a short distance. When within reach the intended victim is seized by a lightning strike of the fore-legs. The harder and more indigestible parts such as the wings are usually discarded. Insects which are too large or which display warning colours (wasps and bees for example) are not usually tackled, although I have seen a hungry mantid catch and eat a large wasp with relish. The victim in this case was firmly held and was unable to sting but I do not know what the result would have been had it been able to do so. They can also be persuaded to catch moths of the family Syntomidae (these have bright colours warning of their distasteful nature) but these are immediately rejected. Presumably these moths are distasteful even to insect predators.

There are reports of mantids attacking small frogs and I have seen a mantis attacking a lizard much larger than itself (Fig 11). In this case the mantis ate a large chunk of flesh from behind the head of the lizard, but the final fate of insect and reptile was not observed. Mantids usually rely on their camouflage for protection but most species will adopt a threatening attitude if provoked, some species standing erect with wings and fore-legs outstretched. They will also strike out with their fore-legs and a large mantid can inflict a painful stab with its tibial spines. The jaws are very powerful too and can draw blood if the insect is handled carelessly.

Fig 12   Mantis egg case – the texture is dry and spongy

The eggs (Fig 12) are laid in batches of about a hundred and as they are laid they are covered with a frothy substance secreted by the female. This hardens quickly to form a tough brown leathery case 2–3 cm long and broad, or less according to the particular species. This case is attached to a branch or twig or sometimes to a wall. The tiny nymphs which emerge look like miniature adults and can jump as well as run. There is usually considerable mortality at this stage, as they will readily consume their less nimble brothers and sisters. The eggs are often parasitised by small wasps and many egg cases will yield only wasps, although not all the eggs in a case are always destroyed.

Fig 11   Mantis (Dictyoptera) eating a small lizard

24

Plate 1   Dragonfly (Odonata)

Plate 2   Damselfly, *Coenagrion* (Odonata)

Plate 3   Bush cricket, family Tettigoniidae (Orthoptera), which
mimics a green leaf

Plate 4   Adult mole-cricket, *Gryllotalpa africana* (Orthoptera)

Plate 5 Adult variegated grasshopper, *Zonocerus* (Orthoptera)

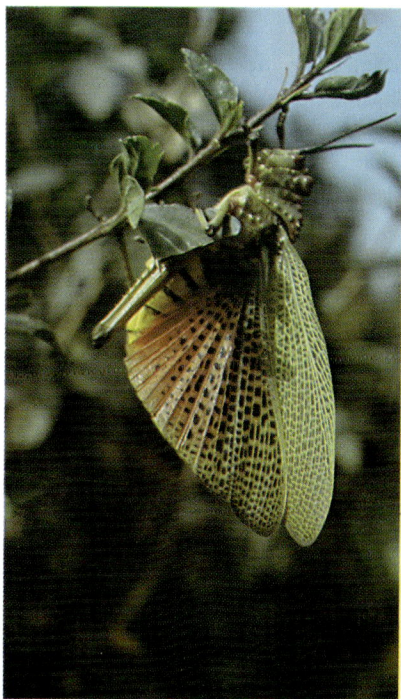

Plate 6 Large grasshopper,
family Acrididae (Orthoptera),
with brightly coloured hind
wings

Plate 7 Scorpion-fly, *Bittacus*
(Mecoptera)

Plate 8   Adult migratory locust, *Locusta migratoria* (Orthoptera)

Plate 9   Three stick insects (Phasmida) resembling dead twigs

Plate 10   Mantis, *Phyllocrania* (Dictyoptera), which mimics a dead
   crumpled leaf

Plate 11   Winged adult termites (Isoptera) attracted to light

Plate 12   Cicada, *Lacetus* (Hemiptera), which mimics a leaf

Plate 13   Scale-insects, family Coccidae (Hemiptera)

Plate 14   Assasin-bug, *Nularda*, family Reduviidae (Hemiptera)

Plate 15   Cocoa capsid bug, *Sahlbergella*, family Miridae (Hemiptera)

Plate 16   Cotton stainer bug, *Dysdercus*, family Pyrrhocoridae
  (Hemiptera)

Plate 17   Shield-bug, family Pentatomidae (Hemiptera)

Plate 18   Giant water bug, *Belostoma*, family Belostomatidae (Hemiptera)

Plate 19   Mantispid, family Mantispidae (Neuroptera) – note the resemblance to a mantis

Plate 20   Adult ant-lion, *Hagenomyia*, family Myrmeleontidae (Neuroptera)

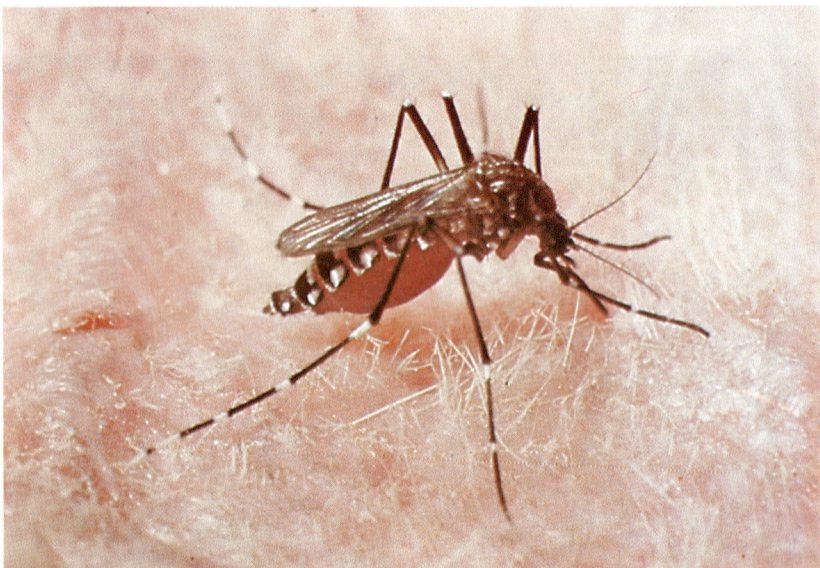

Plate 21   Yellow fever mosquito, *Aedes aegypti*, family Culicidae (Diptera) feeding on the blood of a mouse

Plate 22   Bee-fly, family Bombyliidae (Diptera)

Plate 23   Tsetse fly, *Glossina* (Diptera) – the vector of sleeping
sickness

Plate 24   Driver ants, subfamily Dorylinae (Hymenoptera), attacking a grasshopper

Plate 25   Weaver ants, *Oecophylla*, subfamily Formicinae (Hymenoptera), with their nest in a citrus tree

Plate 26   Hornets, *Polistes*, family Vespidae (Hymenoptera), with
their nest

Plate 27   Tiger beetle, *Megacephala*, family Cicindelidae
(Coleoptera), attacking a grasshopper

Plate 28   *Anthia*, a typical ground-beetle, family Carabidae
(Coleoptera)

Plate 29   Large dung-beetles, *Heliocopris*, family Scarabaeidae
(Coleoptera), each about 5 cm long

Plate 30   Goliath-beetle, family Scarabaeidae (Coleoptera) — one of the largest of all African insects

Plate 31   Beetle of the family Buprestidae (Coleoptera)

Plate 32   Blister-beetle, family Meloidae (Coleoptera)

Plate 33   Longhorn beetle, *Macrotoma*, family Cerambycidae
(Coleoptera)

Isoptera *(Termites)*

The name of this order refers to the adult winged forms, and means 'equal wings' as the fore- and hind-wings are very similar in both appearance and size. They are sometimes referred to as 'white ants' because the workers are white and live in nests in the same fashion as ants, but here the resemblance ends and the name is best discarded for being misleading.

They are social insects and large numbers live together in a common nest. In each community there are several types or castes of individuals. There is a queen (a fertile female whose function is to lay eggs), a king (a fertile male), a large number of workers (sterile males and females, which do the principal tasks of maintaining the colony) and the soldiers (sterile males and females with very powerful jaws and large heads, whose function is to guard the colony). Both workers and soldiers are usually blind, and have no wings.

The eggs which are laid by the queen are carried off to special chambers within the nest and are cared for by the workers. They hatch into tiny white nymphs which resemble minute workers. After several moults they become adult, either reproductive males and females, workers or soldiers. Although there are various theories as to what exactly determines the caste to which the future insect will belong, the exact process is far from being well-understood.

At certain times of the year, usually around the beginning of the rainy season, the fertile adults are produced in large numbers and congregate within the nest. At a certain signal they leave the nest together in large swarms (Plate 11). This signal seems to be a combination of temperature and humidity and the same exodus takes place simultaneously in other nests over a wide area, which ensures interbreeding of the colonies. At this time large numbers of termites are attracted to lights, and they are at their most vulnerable with predators taking a heavy toll.

After a brief mating flight the insects settle and their first act is to snap off their wings at a special joint near the base. The wings have fulfilled their function and are no longer needed; in fact they would be a hindrance rather than a help inside the termite colony. At this stage they can often be seen scurrying about on the ground, head to tail in pairs. If they are fortunate enough to survive all the natural hazards, they seek out a suitable spot to burrow in the ground, or find a suitable hole in which to found a future colony. Here the female starts to lay eggs. At first they live off the accumulated fat reserves in the body or on food other than woody material and the young king and queen termites tend and feed the newly-hatched brood. These are destined to become the first workers of the new colony and when they mature they take over the tasks of constructing the nest and foraging for food.

The queen (Fig 13) then settles down to her main role, that of producing eggs. The

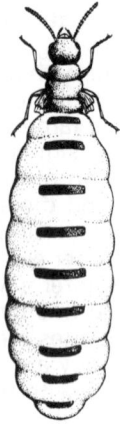

Fig 13   Queen termite (Isoptera)

abdomen of a mature queen swells up to many times its original size and may be as much as 10 cm long. The head and thorax, however, retain their original dimensions although the queen is now so large and heavy that it is impossible for her to move of her own accord. Mature queens may lay up to several thousand eggs each day. Both king and queen are long-lived insects, and may survive for up to fifty years. Most of the large nests that one sees are many years old.

   Most termite nests (Fig 14) are built of chewed soil mixed with saliva, a mixture which is often extremely hard. Some species build nests which are entirely subterranean, but usually a part is above ground with the major portion below surface level. Some species build very large mounds which may be as much as 2–3 m high. Some species in the forest regions build nests which have overhanging caps and which look like large mushrooms; the caps presumably

act as a sort of rain shield. Some species make their nests in trees, attached to large branches. The presence of such nests is often indicated by 'run-ways' covered with chewed wood and soil on the trunk of a tree. Inside the nest there are numerous galleries and tunnels and if a hole is made in the nest soldiers flock to the breach and guard it while the damage is made good in an astonishingly short time by the workers. Deep within the nest, usually about two-thirds down is the royal cell in which the king and queen termites live. This is a completely enclosed chamber just large enough to contain the king, the queen and a few workers. There are entrance holes large enough for the workers but far too small for the queen who is a virtual prisoner inside.

Fig 14   Termite mound (about 1 m high) with overhanging caps

Termites feed on a variety of vegetable matter, mainly of a dry woody nature. Many species of termites are unable to digest the cellulose and lignin which are the main constituents of their woody diet, since they do not possess the necessary digestive enzymes to do so. They solve this difficulty by acting as host within their gut to enormous numbers of micro-organisms (protozoa and bacteria) which obligingly break down these plant constituents into a form in which they can be utilised by the termites. Newly hatched nymphs do not possess these micro-organisms, but are infected by the workers by being fed termite excreta which is contaminated with the organisms. The future queen also carries a supply of these organisms to pass on to her offspring when she founds a new colony.

Some types of termites are fungus-feeders, the fungus being grown and harvested within special chambers within the nest. They collect and feed upon wood or dried grass or other woody materials. This is chewed up but only partly digested, since they do not possess the wood-digesting protozoa in their gut. Their excreta is collected and is used as a basis on which to grow special types of fungi within the galleries of the nest. The fungus is carefully tended by the worker termites and the fruiting bodies are used as food for both the adults and the developing nymphs. These 'fungus gardens' can easily be seen if a nest is broken open, the fungus appearing as pin-head sized white balls dotted about here and there within the galleries of the nest.

Soldier termites (Fig 15) use their very powerful mandibles for defence of the nest. The much enlarged head-capsule accommodates powerful muscles for the jaws and they are capable of giving a painful bite if annoyed. In certain species the soldiers have modified heads which are drawn out into a long 'snout'. These are termed 'nasute' forms; their heads contain a gland which secretes a repellent sticky fluid which they are able to squirt at any invaders. Ants are probably the main insect enemies of termites, especially the driver ants.

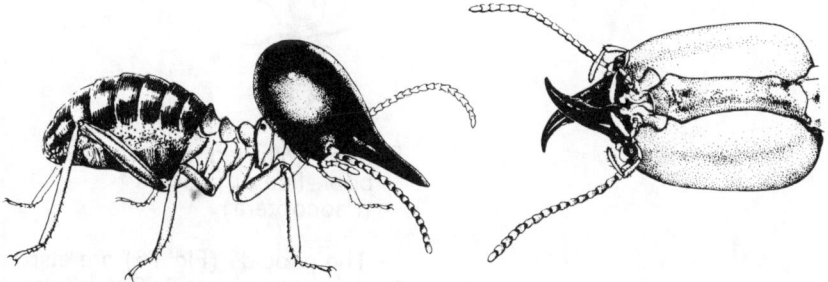

Fig 15   Soldier termites — the nasute form (left) and head and jaws of a typical soldier (right)

43

Because of their habit of eating wood, termites are of great economic importance for the damage they can cause to buildings and house timbers. This is especially so as the termites can tunnel unseen within timbers and the damage may not be appreciated until structural failure occurs. They are important pests of stored crops, particularly yams and maize, and they are also known to attack young cocoa and other growing plants. In contrast to this they can be valuable allies of man since their activities break up vegetable matter and carry it into the soil, improving its texture and allowing rain to penetrate. In forest areas termites break down fallen trees and branches, allowing their contained nutrients to be returned to the soil and recycled. This aspect is also of great importance in pasture land, particularly in savannah areas.

Zoraptera and Psocoptera (Psocids or Book-lice)

The Zoraptera (there is no common name) are minute insects less than 3 mm long which have been found under bark, in rotting wood and also in termite nests. They are usually without wings although some winged forms have been described, but these are thought to be of rare occurrence. They have stout nine-segmented antennae. Fewer than twenty species are known in West Africa and Asia and very little is known of their life-history, although the nymphs are said to resemble the adults. They are of no economic importance.

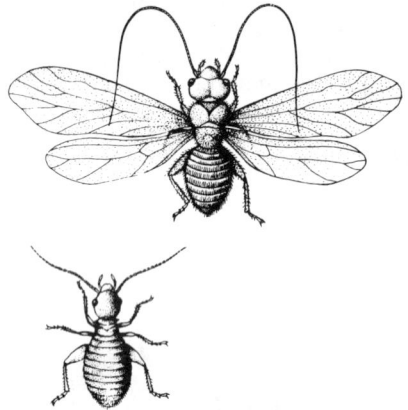

Fig 16   Winged and wingless book-lice or psocids (Psocoptera)

The psocids (Fig 16) are also tiny insects, about 2—3 mm long. Many species are without wings but some, particularly those

which live out-of-doors, have
two pairs of wings with a very
characteristic venation. The
mouthparts are adapted for
chewing and biting and they
feed on a variety of organic
matter particularly fungi and
algae. They are often found
indoors, in larders or among
collections of old papers or books
(hence the name 'book-lice').
Outdoors they are found under
bark and in birds' nests and may
be attracted to light at night.
Some species are semi-colonial,
numbers being found together
under a canopy of silken threads.
In some, reproduction is by
parthenogenesis, the males being
unknown. When present in large
numbers they may constitute a
nuisance, but otherwise they are
of no economic concern. They
are particularly fond of dead
insects and may infest insect
collections, so they are no
friends of the entomologist.

Mallophaga and Siphunculata *(Lice)*

These two orders of insects are
parasitic on animals and birds;
they are without wings and live
among the hairs or feathers of
the host.

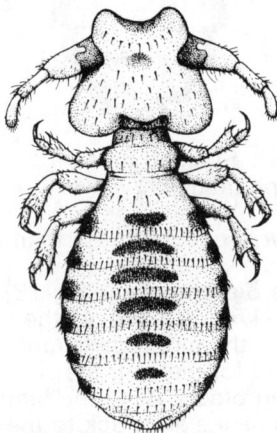

Fig 17   Biting louse
(Mallophaga)

The Mallophaga (Fig 17) are
the biting lice, with mouthparts
which are modified for chewing
and biting. They are mostly
found on birds and most species
are host-specific — a certain
species of louse is confined to a
certain host species. A few are
found on mammals, for example
on dogs and cattle, but they are
not found on humans. They live
by feeding on fragments of
feather or hair, and skin scales.
The eggs are cemented to a
feather or hair and the nymphs
which hatch are like small
editions of the adult. The whole

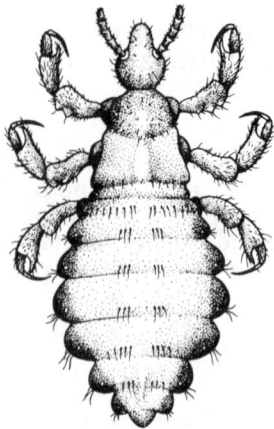

Fig 18   Sucking louse
(Siphunculata)

life-cycle occupies less than a month.

The Siphunculata (Fig 18) are the sucking lice and, as the name implies, the mouthparts are adapted for piercing the skin and sucking blood. As in the biting lice the eggs are stuck to the hairs of the host and both adults and nymphs have well-developed claws by which they cling on to the hairs. The most notorious of the lice are *Pediculus*, the human body and head louse, and *Pthirus*, the human crab-louse. Pigs and cattle are frequently infested with their own particular species of louse.

The activities of both of these types of lice cause intense irritation to the host. Domestic fowls are commonly infested with the biting louse *Menopon gallinae*. Infested birds scratch and peck each other and there is a severe loss of egg production. The activities of the sucking lice are even more serious since they are capable of acting as vectors of a numbers of diseases of man. These include epidemic typhus (caused by a Rickettsia), murine typhus (normally carried by fleas, but which may be louse-borne) and relapsing fever (caused by a Spirochaete).

Hemiptera *(Bugs)*

In many ways this is one of the most remarkable and most diverse of all the orders of insects. It is of great significance to man since it includes species that transmit virus and other diseases of plants, animals and man, and many important primary pests of crops. Its members are distinguished by having a proboscis which is modified for piercing and sucking. This proboscis has fine stylets which are inserted into the tissues of the host plant or animal to introduce saliva and to withdraw sap or blood. It is usually held folded back beneath the head when not in use and is then not visible from above. The order is divided into two main suborders: the Homoptera, in which both the fore- and hind-wings are membranous and are usually held sloping over the sides of the body, like a roof; and the Heteroptera, in which the fore-wing has the basal half thickened and the outer half membranous. In some bugs the wings have been lost through adaptation to a sedentary or parasitic habit.

The life-cycle is typically of the egg — nymph — adult type, although many variations occur. Many aphids, for instance, are viviparous, and some scale-insects are parthenogenetic. Some aphids have even more complex life-cycles, where oviparous sexual forms alternate with viviparous parthenogenetic forms. Many bugs, particularly those belonging to the Homoptera, (for example aphids, tree-hoppers and mealybugs) have developed associations with ants. Since the bugs feed on plant juices, which contain much sugar but little protein, large volumes of sap must be taken in. The excess fluid is excreted as a sugary substance known as 'honeydew'. Colonies of bugs are protected and tended by ants and in return the bugs extrude from the anus drops of honeydew which are eagerly imbibed by the ants. In some cases the honeydew is produced when the ants 'milk' the bugs by caressing them with their antennae. There are many families of bugs, but lack of space means that only a brief mention of the most interesting of them can be given here. The various families of the Homoptera will be dealt with first.

One family which must be familiar to all who have lived in any but the most desert regions of the tropics, by sound if not by sight, is the cicada (family Cicadidae). The adults (Plate 12) are handsome insects, up to 5 cm long and one common species is mainly green with silver and black markings. The nymphs live below ground, feeding on the roots of trees and shrubs, often for many years (in one species found in the U.S.A. the nymphs take 17 years to develop). When mature they come to the surface and crawl up the trunk of a tree where the empty nymphal skins may sometimes be seen attached to the bark. The adults are strong fliers and are often attracted to lights at night. Only the males make the high-pitched buzzing noise, which is produced by a drum-like muscle-operated chitinous membrane vibrating over a hollow sounding-chamber beneath the first segment of the abdomen. It is most difficult to locate the adults by sound and even when detected they are very alert and if approached will quickly move round to the other side of the trunk or branch on which they are sitting. Cicada nymphs may cause damage to some plants by their tunnelling and feeding but they are not usually of any economic significance.

The cuckoo-spit insects or frog-hoppers (family Cercopidae) are common on a variety of plants and the adults, which are about 1 cm long, are often brightly coloured in scarlet and black. The nymphs surround themselves with a frothy secretion which is said to protect them from the sun and from drying. They can cause damage to cultivated plants by feeding on their sap and thus affecting their growth.

Tree-hoppers (family Membracidae) present a most curious appearance. They are usually small, about $\frac{1}{2}$ cm long,

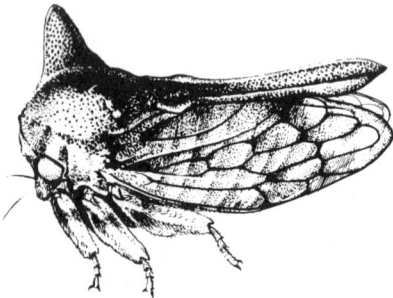

Fig 19   Membracid bug, family
    Membracidae (Hemiptera)

and have leaf-like projections on the prothorax (Fig 19). They are found in colonies on the shoots of trees and bushes and the colonies are often tended by ants. The nymphs are very like the adults in appearance, but have

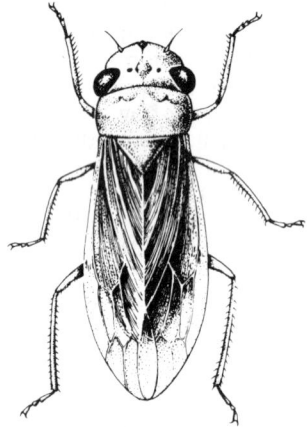

Fig 20   Leaf-hopper bug, family
    Cicadellidae (Hemiptera)

smaller thoracic ornaments.

Leaf-hoppers (Fig 20) or jassid bugs (family Cicadellidae) are among the most abundant of all bugs on grasses and on other vegetation, and they can jump appreciable distances if disturbed. They are important pests of rice and other crops and can transmit a variety of plant viruses. They also cause serious stunting of growth by feeding on the plant tissues and causing mechanical damage. Very occasionally they will attempt to bite humans (presumably by mistake) and then their bite is quite painful but not serious.

Bugs belonging to the family Flattidae (they do not have a common name) are beautiful

Fig 21   Flattid bug nymph,
family Flattidae (Hemiptera) —
the long waxy hairs are fluffed
out when the insect is
disturbed

moth-like insects about 2 cm
long and coloured green and red
or pink. They are most often
found in groups on plants but are
occasionally attracted to lights at
night. The nymphs (Fig 21) are
also found in groups and they
are covered in long waxy white

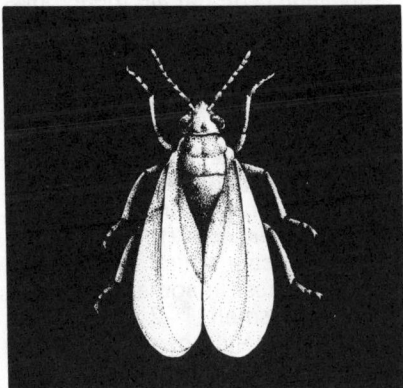

Fig 22   Whitefly, family
Aleurodidae (Hemiptera) —
resemble small moths

filaments which wave about in
the breeze, and which they can
fluff out if disturbed.

Members of the family
Aleurodidae (Fig 22) or whiteflies
are minute insects measuring only
about 2–3 mm long and the
adults look like miniature white-
winged moths. Both the wings
and body are covered with a
white waxy powder which repels
water and this makes them very
difficult to kill by spraying with
ordinary water-based insecticides.
They are found in large numbers
on the undersides of leaves and
stems of infested plants and the
adults fly readily if disturbed.
The nymphs resemble minute oval
greenish scales and have only
rudimentary legs and antennae
and they do not move. The adults
fly freely from plant to plant and
in doing so they can transmit
plant viruses. They are common
on cassava, tomatoes, peppers
and on many other plants.
Cassava mosaic virus is an
important disease transmitted by
whiteflies.

Greenfly (Fig 23) or aphids
(family Aphididae) are notorious
cosmopolitan pests. They cause
considerable damage by feeding
on plant sap and they are also
important vectors of a variety of
plant virus diseases. For example,
Aphis gosypii is an important
pest of cotton, and groundnut
rosette virus is transmitted by
aphids. An interesting effect of
aphids infestation occurs on
sorghum. When aphids are
present in large numbers the
leaves become attractive to cattle
and the leaves may be grazed off
infested plants.

The biology of aphids is

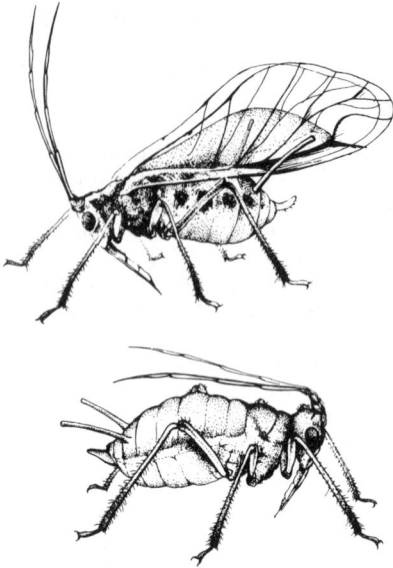

Fig 23   Winged and wingless
aphids, family Aphididae
(Hemiptera)

complex, and there are many
variations on the following
theme. Eggs, laid by sexually
mature females, hatch to give rise
to wingless adults which are
viviparous and reproduce
parthenogenetically. These give
rise to further wingless
generations, but among these
some winged forms may be
produced, which are also
parthenogenetic and viviparous.
The winged forms disperse to
other plants and set up new
infestations. At certain times of
the year sexual generations are
produced. the males and females
mate and the females lay eggs
which eventually hatch to start
the cycle over again. Some aphids
have very marked migratory
habits and some may spend part

of the year on one species of
plant and the rest on another
quite different plant. Colonies of
aphids usually consist of mixed
winged and wingless individuals.

Viviparous aphids can produce
two or three nymphs each day
and since the nymphs themselves
only take a few days to mature
each aphid has the potential to
give rise to an enormous number
of individuals in a very short time.
Fortunately aphids have several
important natural enemies
including lacewings, ladybird
beetles and the larvae of hover
flies. Ants are frequently
associated with aphids. Some
aphids secrete a white waxy
substance which coats their
bodies and a number of species
live below ground, feeding on the
roots of plants.

The Coccidae (or more strictly
the superfamily Coccoidea, the
mealybugs and scale-insects) do
not look like insects at all at
first sight. The males of these
insects are winged but are only
rarely seen. The female mealybugs
are covered with a white waxy
secretion and the scale insects
are covered with a hard 'scale'
composed of the nymphal skin
hardened with a resinous
substance (Plate 13). The female
bugs are degenerate with no
wings and only poorly developed
legs. Scale-insects (for instance
the citrus scale which is an
important pest in some areas)
are usually small, 1–2 mm across,
but some mealybugs may measure
2–3 cm if one counts the waxy
coat as 'insect'. When this coat
is removed, for example if it is
dissolved away in a solvent like
petrol, the actual bug is seen to

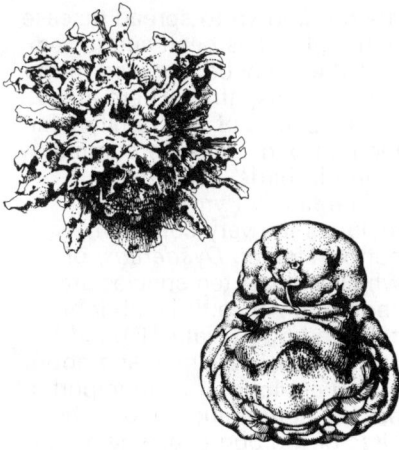

Fig 24   Mealybug, family
    Coccidae (Hemiptera), with
    its waxy coat and the bug with
    the wax removed

be only about half this size
(Fig 24). These bugs infest a
wide variety of crops including
citrus, coffee, cocoa and sugar
cane, and are serious agricultural
pests. Mealybugs transmit a
variety of plant virus diseases,
one of the most important of
which in West Africa is cocoa
swollen shoot disease virus.
There is often a complex
association between populations
of mealybugs and ants (see
page 71).

    We now come to the families
which belong to the suborder
Heteroptera. Assassin-bugs
(Plate 14), which belong to the
family Reduviidae are mostly
predatory on other insects
although some bite animals
including man. Some species of
assassin-bugs prey upon the
common pest the cotton-stainer
bugs (see page 52). They have

a short stout proboscis and many
species (even the insect-hunting
ones) will give a painful bite if
handled carelessly. They are often
brightly coloured and many are
large insects, more than 2–3 cm
long. It is a very diverse family
in West Africa and there are also
species which are very slender
and resemble mosquitoes, on
which they feed. Some species
camouflage themselves by
covering their bodies with debris.
The eggs are large and laid
singly and the nymphs have the
same habits as the adults.

    Adults of the family Gerridae
or pond-skaters are almost 2 cm
long when fully grown. They are
a familiar sight on the surface of
ponds and slow-flowing streams,
where they glide about effortlessly
over the surface. The legs and
body are clothed with water-
repelling hairs, and the insect is
so light that it is able to support
itself on the surface film by the
mid- and hind-legs. The front
pair of legs is reduced in size
and is held tucked up below the
thorax and is used for grasping
dead or live insects that fall into
the water and on which the bugs
feed. The eggs are laid on water
plants and the nymphs resemble
the adults but have no wings.
The adults are good fliers and in
this manner make their way from
pond to pond. The family also
contains a number of wingless
forms which are found on the
surface of the sea, sometimes
very many miles from land.

    Capsid bugs (Plate 15), which
belong to the family Miridae,
are usually small, less than 1 cm
long, and live by sucking sap
from the tender shoots of plants.

They are important pests because the saliva injected by the bug when it sucks sap is toxic to the plant tissues and causes stunting and deformation of the tissues. This in turn may lead to infections with fungus diseases. Capsid bugs are particularly important pests of cocoa, especially the

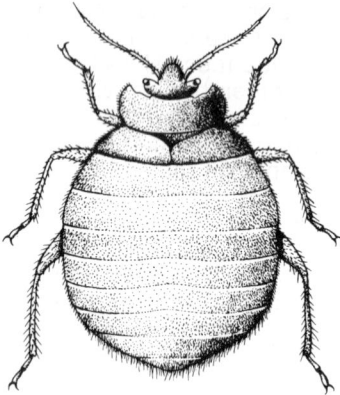

Fig 25   Bed-bug, family
          Cimicidae (Hemiptera)

species *Sahlbergella* and *Helopeltis*.

The notorious bed-bug (Fig 25) belongs to the family Cimicidae. When unfed, they are flat brown oval creatures about 3–5 mm long with an objectionable oily smell. They do not possess wings. They feed on blood and are nocturnal, hiding in cracks or crevices in walls or furniture during the day. Overcrowded, dirty conditions favour infestations by bed-bugs and sometimes the extent of the problem cannot be seen unless a search is made by night when the bugs emerge from their hiding-places. Despite being found in close association with man, they are not known to spread disease, although it has been suggested that they may be involved in the spread of hepatitis. There are some species of this family which feed on birds, and are commonly found in birds' nests.

The family Pyrrhocoridae includes the very common cotton-stainer, *Dysdercus*, of which at least ten species are known in Africa. It is a brightly coloured bug (Plate 16), red with brown markings, and about 1–1.5 cm long. It is an important pest of cotton and kapok. The bites of the bug cause damage to the unripe cotton bolls which then become infected with fungus. This fungus develops in the boll, staining it and reducing the quality and value of the crop. The bugs may also be found in very large numbers on baobab trees, on silk-cotton and kapok (*Ceiba* and *Bombax*) and also on okra plants. The adult bugs are unable to reproduce unless they are able to feed from the seeds of these plants (which belong to the plant family Malvaceae), although they can live by sucking from the vegetative shoots; presumably they extract from the seeds some factor needed for reproduction.

The Coreidae (which have no common name) are medium to large bugs but usually less than 2 cm long. They may be brown or green in colour and some species have extraordinary leaf-like expansions of the antennae, legs and body. They are very important pests of legumes in West Africa. The bug *Acanthomia*, for instance, is a pest of the cowpea, feeding on the seeds and causing extensive damage to the crop.

The Pentatomidae (shield-bugs or stink-bugs) give off a foul odour when crushed as glands in the abdomen secrete a foul-smelling fluid which provides protection from most predators (Plate 17). They sometimes occur in savannah areas in such numbers as to become a major pest. *Carbula pedalis*, for example, occasionally occurs in houses in such numbers that the occupants are forced to leave and in some cases the infestations have been so bad that houses have had to be burned down to get rid of the bugs. The eggs of shield-bugs are laid on plants in small batches and in a few cases the female bugs have been seen to guard the eggs and newly hatched nymphs in much the same fashion as earwigs. The nymphs are often differently coloured from the adults. Most of the species feed on plants, but some are predaceous on other insects and particularly on butterfly larvae. The bug *Bathycoelia* has recently become a major pest of cocoa in West Africa.

The largest of the West African bugs belongs to the family Belostomatidae (giant water-bugs). They live in pools or streams (Plate 18), usually in the mud on the bottom or on water plants, but they are more usually seen at night when they fly and are attracted to lights. They are quite good fliers and make their way from one pool to the next in this way. They may reach 8–10 cm in length but are very ungainly creatures on dry land. The fore-legs have large spines with which they are able to catch and hold their prey – water insects, frogs, tadpoles and even small fish. They can give a painful bite if handled carelessly. In some species the eggs are attached to the back of the male by the female, and he carries them about with him until they hatch.

The last two families of bugs we shall mention here are the Notonectidae (the backswimmers) and the Corixidae (the water-boatmen). Both of these, as their names suggest, live in water although they can, and do, fly. They measure up to 1–2 cm long. Backswimmers, as might be expected, swim on their backs, which are shaped like the keel of a boat and they are often to be seen floating on their backs just at the surface, ready to dive if disturbed. Water-boatmen (Fig 26) swim dorsal side up and the dorsal side of the body is flattened. In both, the abdomen is flattened under the wing cases, forming a cavity in which a bubble of air is trapped and

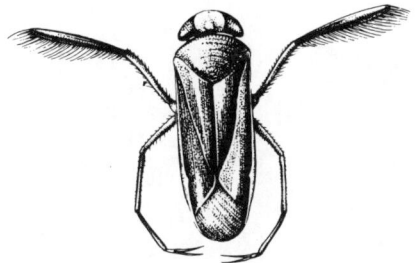

Fig 26   Water-boatman, family Corixidae (Hemiptera) – the middle legs have a frings of long hairs and act as paddles

which is used for respiration when submerged. The bug renews its air supply when it surfaces by thrusting the hind end of its body through the surface film. Backswimmers are predaceous and feed on other aquatic insects, tadpoles and small fish. They will give a nasty bite if handled carelessly. Water-boatmen feed on algae and small water plants. Neither are of any economic importance.

Thysanoptera *(Thrips)*

These are small to minute yellow, orange, dark brown or black insects (Fig 27) with two pairs of feather-like wings which have very long fringes of hairs. They are usually to be found in large numbers on flowers or leaves on which they feed by rasping at the epidermis with their mouth-parts. A few of the species are known to be predaceous, feeding on other thrips.

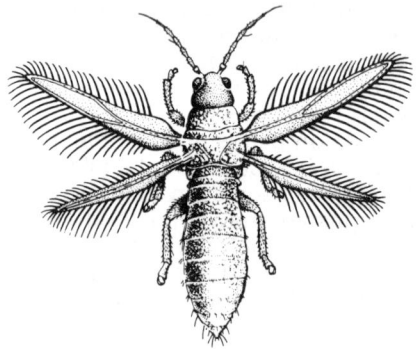

Fig 27   Adult thrip (Thysanoptera) — very small insects
usually less than 2 mm long

The eggs are laid on plants and the nymphs which hatch from them undergo four moults before becoming adult. The fourth stage is unusual in that it is a semi-resting stage resembling in many ways the pupa of those insects with a complete metamor-phosis, such as butterflies. It has long wing-pads and is usually motionless although it can move slowly if disturbed, but it does not feed.

Thrips may be pests when present in large numbers, doing considerable damage to growing plants and crops. Some are of particular importance as vectors of virus diseases of plants. They have recently become recognised as important pests of legumes, cocoa and cashew and much work has been done in Nigeria on their biology. *Taeniothrips* is a pest of cowpea and *Selenothrips* is a pest of cocoa and cashew; both of these species cause serious mechanical damage by their feeding activities to flowers, leaves and fruit.

Neuroptera (Lacewings, Mantispids, Ascalaphids and Ant-lions)

This order consists mainly of rather delicate-looking insects with long, thin bodies and two pairs of fragile, often transparent wings. These have a fine network of veins which form a large number of rectangular or polygonal cells. They could easily be mistaken — and indeed often are mistaken — for dragonflies or damselflies, but they have much longer and more prominent antennae than those insects.

Lacewings are an assemblage of several families with the same general pattern of rather delicate broad wings and long thread-like antennae. They are green or brown in colour and often have beautiful iridescent golden-coloured eyes. The eggs are laid in batches on leaves, and each egg is attached to the leaf by a long stalk secreted by the female. The larvae are greenish or blackish in colour, and are short and broad with three pairs of prominent legs and a formidable pair of hollow jaws. They feed mainly on aphids which are pierced by the jaws and the body contents sucked out. In many lacewings the remains of the victims are stuck on the body spines of the larva, camouflaging it effectively. Lacewing adults also feed upon aphids.

The mantispids (family Mantispidae) are easily separated from other Neuroptera by the structure of the fore-legs which are adapted for catching and holding other insects in exactly the same way as those of mantids. Indeed, they are so like small mantids that careful inspection is often needed to distinguish them, but they may be separated by the fact that both pairs of wings in the mantispid are similar in shape and venation, and that the antennae are short and only two or three times longer than the head (Plate 19). In mantids the antennae are very long. They are not large insects, being less than 4 cm across the wings and they are brown or green in colour. They are active at night and are often attracted to bright lights. Their life-history is particularly interesting. The eggs are laid on leaves, twigs or stones and are raised above the surface on which they are laid by short stalks. When the larva hatches it seeks out and burrows into the egg cocoon of a spider (some species of mantispid prey on wasps). A single larvae enters each cocoon and feeds upon the unhatched eggs and on any young spiders. When fully grown, by which time it has destroyed all the spider's eggs, it spins a cocoon of silk around itself and pupates within the last larval skin, so that the adult which finally emerges has to pierce its own larval skin, its own cocoon and the egg-cocoon of the spider in order to free itself.

The Nemopteridae (they have no common name) is a family of very striking insects which are unlikely to be mistaken for any other, as the hind-wings are very narrow, long and ribbon-like (Fig 28). Very little is known of

Fig 28   Adult of the family Nemopteridae (Neuroptera)

the West African species, but one that I have seen was some 5 cm across the fore-wings and had hind-wings about 10 cm long. They are said to fly with a curious up-and-down motion. The larvae are predaceous and feed on small insects such as psocids. They are often found indoors.

The Ascalaphidae (Fig 29) are fairly common in savannah regions and may often be seen by day hawking up and down paths like dragonflies, in search of insects which they capture on the wing. They are quite large insects, mostly around 5 cm across, and many species have coloured wings. The chief

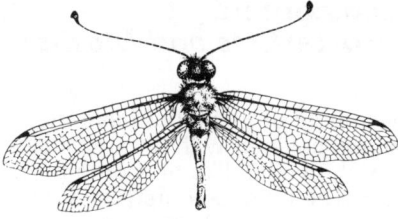

Fig 29   Ascalaphid fly, family
    Ascalaphidae (Neuroptera)

distinguishing feature is the
antennae which are very long
(almost as long as the wings)
and are clubbed at the ends. The
larvae are very like those of the
ant-lions, but they do not make
pits.

Ant-lions (Plate 20), which
belong to the family
Myrmeleontidae, are generally
common but seldom seen.
Many readers must have noticed
small conical pits in the dry,
sandy soil under the eaves of
buildings, near to the wall
where the rain cannot drip
down. They may be 1—5 cm
deep, by the same amount across,

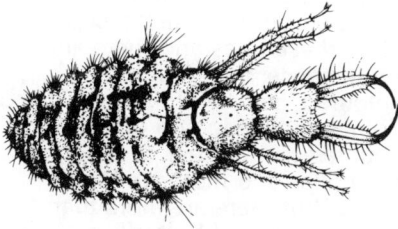

Fig 30   Larva of an ant-lion,
    family Myrmeleontidae
    (Neuroptera)

and are made by the larvae of
ant-lions.

The eggs are laid in loose
sandy soil and the larvae which
hatch from them are fearsome-
looking creatures (Fig 30),
with oval-shaped spiny bodies
and a massive pair of hollow jaws
projecting from the front of the
head. It is with these jaws that
they capture and suck the juices
of their prey. They construct their
pits by burrowing backwards in
the soil in circles, flicking away
loose soil to one side with their
jaws. In this way a conical pit
is made in a very short time.
The larva hides just below
the soil level at the bottom
of the pit. If an ant or other small
insect stumbles into the pit it
falls to the bottom and has
difficulty in escaping because of
the loose dry soil on the sides of
the pit. In addition, the ant-lion
larva flicks up more soil to knock
the insect back to the bottom.
When the victim becomes
exhausted in its efforts to escape,
or comes within range, it is seized
and dragged below the surface
and when it has been sucked dry
the empty carcase is pushed out.

When fully grown, the larva
forms a small cell below ground
and pupates; the head, wings and
legs of the future adult can
clearly be seen. The adults are
active at night and have a slow,
flapping flight. I have seen the
adults of one large species
measuring 9 cm on roads in
eastern Nigeria at night. Their
eyes shone like small red jewels
in the headlights of a car and
could easily have been mistaken
for the eyes of a small animal or
bird.

Mecoptera
(Scorpion-flies)

This order includes some uncommon insects which are not
often noticed unless one is on
the lookout for them. The head of
the adult is prolonged downwards
to form a sort of beak which
bears the biting mouthparts. The
adults are predaceous and live on
other insects. They have a
distinct pupal stage and the
larvae, which are said to resemble
caterpillars, live in the soil.

Bittacus (Plate 7) is the
representative of the group most
likely to be encountered. It is
about 2.5 cm long, brownish
orange in colour with two pairs
of clear wings and very long legs.
It looks like a crane-fly but these
have only one pair of wings. They
are usually to be found resting on
vegetation, hanging on to a stem
or twig by the fore-legs, with
the hind-legs trailing. The hind-
legs are unusual in that the last
joint can fold up on the one
before like the blade of a penknife
and by this means any insects
which come within reach are
seized and eaten.

The name 'scorpion-fly' is a
reference to some of the species
from temperate climates, which
rest with the end of the abdomen
held doubled over on the insect's
back, rather like a scorpion.
Although they look fearsome they
do not bite or sting, and are of
no economic or medical
significance to man.

Lepidoptera
(Butterflies and Moths)

Members of this order have the
wings covered with minute scales
which overlap like tiles on a roof,
and which are coloured. It is the
arrangement of these coloured
scales which makes the beautiful
patterns on the wings.

The order will only be
mentioned briefly here, since it
has already been dealt with in a
separate volume of the present
series. There is no hard and fast
distinction between butterflies
and moths, save that the term
'butterfly' is given to a group of
families of the Lepidoptera, and
the 'moths' are the remainder. In
general butterflies fly by day and
moths by night; butterflies have
antennae which end in a distinct
club, whereas moth antennae
have various forms; and butterflies
rest with their wings folded over
their backs (and have the
undersides of the wings
camouflaged), whereas most
moths rest with their wings
folded over the body and are
camouflaged on the upper surface. Many moths too are dull-
coloured but there are exceptions
to all these rules and there are,
for instance, many brightly-
coloured, day-flying moths.
To my knowledge no one has
counted the number of kinds of
butterflies and moths in West
Africa, but there are more than
1,000 species of butterflies
and perhaps 10,000 species of
moths. Butterflies vary in size
from about 1 cm (some of the
small 'blues', family Lycaenidae)
to the handsome reddish-orange

and black *Papilio antimachus* (family Papilionidae, the 'swallow-tails') which spans almost 25 cm and is the largest butterfly found in Africa. Moths vary from minute (some of the leaf-miners are less than 3 mm across) to the hawk-moths (12 cm) and the emperor moths (20 cm).

In some species the males and females have quite different colour patterns on the wings, while in others the sexes are similar. Some have differently coloured forms in the wet and dry seasons. The enormous range of size and colour patterns, combined with their permanence when the insects are killed, dried and stored properly, makes this order a favourite with collectors.

Many butterflies are attracted to flowers and can be captured (or, better, photographed) while feeding on nectar. Some may be found congregating in large numbers around puddles on forest paths or on the banks of streams. Over-ripe fruit or dead, decomposing animals are a powerful lure for some species. Many moths are attracted to light and flowers. If you visit a flame tree which is in flower at dusk you will almost always see numbers of hawk-moths hovering over the flowers, and the flowers of the male pawpaw tree are very attractive to dusk-flying 'skipper' butterflies. Most Lepidoptera adults feed on nectar, but some do not feed at all at this stage. Some species of noctuid moths have a very short proboscis with which they pierce and suck ripe fruit.

The life-history consists of egg, larva, pupa and adult. The eggs are laid singly or in batches on or near plants, and the larvae usually feed on the leaves. Some bore into the stems of plants, or into the wood of trees and the larvae of leaf-miner moths burrow between the upper and lower surfaces of leaves. In most species the larval stage occupies anything from a few days to a month or so, but some moths whose larvae bore into trees may spend a year or two as larvae. The pupae are formed on the food-plant or below ground and many moths spin a silken cocoon before they pupate. The pupal stage is variable in duration, from a week or two to several months. The adults may live for only a few days or for several months.

The larvae of some moths are of great economic importance because of the damage they cause to crops and to stored products. The larva of the moth *Maruca*, for example, is an important pest of cowpea and the larvae of other species bore into the stems of maize or into the pods of cocoa. Some larvae have stinging hairs which can cause an unpleasant rash if they are handled carelessly, but none are of major medical importance.

Silk from the cocoons of some moths is used commercially for the production of cloth. Species of the families Saturniidae (emperor moths), Lasiocampidae (the silkworm moth *Bombyx mori* belongs to this family) and Thaumetopoeidae are used in this way. The cocoons of the latter family are used in West Africa. The adult moth,

Anaphe species, is white with dark brown markings. Two species are mainly of value for their silk: *A. infracta* produces a brown silk and *A. imbrasia* yields a white silk. The larvae live communally under a web of silk woven on the food-plant, a shrub called *Bridelia*, and when mature the larvae spin cocoons within the web. The silk cannot be reeled off in a single thread as in the silk-worm since it is not produced in continuous lengths and having been spun by many individuals it is impossible to unravel. It can be spun, however, and it is very strong. The cocoons contain fragments of hair from the larvae which can cause intense irritation in sensitive people, but these are removed during the processing of the silk. The larvae of both of these species are also popular as items of food in some parts of West Africa. Robes made of silk are much valued and at one time the wearing of such robes was the prerogative of natural rulers and their courts.

Trichoptera *(Caddis-flies)*

At first sight a caddis-fly (Fig 31) could easily be mistaken for a moth, but a close examination of the wings will show them to be clothed with hairs, not scales as in the butterflies and moths.

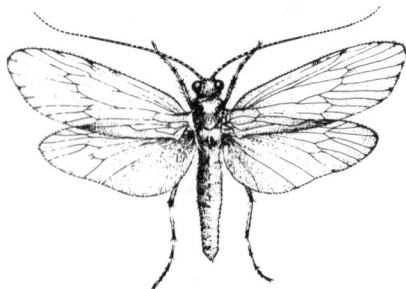

Fig 31   Caddis-fly (Trichoptera)

There are two pairs of long, narrow wings, the antennae are long and thread-like and the adults have no proboscis and only vestigial mouthparts. Most species take no food as adults. They are most active at night and are often attracted to lights in large numbers especially near streams. Most species are brown or dull greyish in colour.

The early stages are aquatic. The eggs are laid in batches in water on rocks or on water plants. When the larva hatches it makes a shelter or case for itself of silk, which it covers with grains of sand, pieces of stick or fragments of vegetation. The type of material used is often characteristic of the particular family of caddis-flies. The larva rests within the case anchored by hooks at the end of the body and when it moves or feeds, it takes its case with it. The case is enlarged at each moult. The pupa is formed within the case and has the legs and wings free from the body. It often has a pair of jaws which are used in freeing the pupa from the larval case, but not for feeding. Just prior to emergence the pupa crawls up to the surface and the adult emerges into the air above.

Although some species may occasionally occur in large enough numbers to cause a nuisance they cannot be rated as pests. They will not breed in polluted water.

Diptera *(Flies)*

Most insects have two pairs of · wings but in some, both pairs have been reduced or lost during the course of evolution. In the Diptera, the hind pair of wings has been reduced to a pair of small, club-like structures. These are called halteres, and act as a kind of gyroscopic balancing organ. A number of Diptera, that are specialised parasites of bats and birds, have lost their wings altogether. In most flies the wings are clear, although the wing membrane may sometimes be coloured or patterned and some have small hairs or scales along the veins and the margins of the wings.

Flies have a complete metamorphosis of the egg – larva – pupa – adult type but there is an enormous variation in detail between species. Thus the larvae of some are terrestrial, some are aquatic, and yet others are parasitic, living within the bodies of other insects and of vertebrates including mammals. The larvae are legless, as for example the familiar 'maggots' in rotting meat which are the larvae of 'blow-flies'. Most larvae lack a well-defined head, although the larvae of members of the first section of the order have distinct heads. The pupa may be formed free or may be covered by the hardened skin of the larva, forming a characteristic brown cylindrical puparium.

It is probably true to say that flies have caused more misery and disease among man and domestic animals than any other group of creatures, other perhaps than man himself. For among them are found the insects which transmit diseases of man such as malaria, yellow fever, filariasis, sleeping sickness and many other diseases of animals. Other flies are important pests of crops and are responsible for the annual destruction of large amounts of agricultural produce. The order is divided by entomologists into three sections or sub-orders, the Nematocera, the Brachycera, and the Cyclorrapha. These are separated on many details of structure, but broadly speaking members of the Nematocera have long thread-like antennae and larvae with distinct heads, while members of the other two sub-orders are more stoutly-built flies with short antennae of fewer segments than in the Nematocera. The Diptera is a very large order indeed, and it is only possible to deal with a few of the families here. The details of the biology of many species of flies is unknown and a study of the flies would prove most rewarding to the amateur and student entomologist alike.

In the Nematocera, the first family which we will deal with is the Tipulidae (crane-flies). These are medium to large flies which may measure up to 5–6 cm across the wings and have very long delicate legs (Fig 32). They may often be found in numbers at the bottom of tree trunks, especially those with buttressed roots and some species constantly bob up and down on their long legs. The larvae are commonly known as 'leather-jackets' on account of their leathery appearance. They are found in the

Fig 32   Crane-fly, family Tipulidae (Diptera)

soil and feed on the roots of plants, causing considerable damage to crops if present in large numbers. Female crane-flies often have a prominent horny ovipositor which looks like a formidable sting, but they neither sting nor bite and do not transmit any diseases of animals.

The next family, the Culicidae, comprises the all-too-familiar mosquitoes. The eggs are laid on the surface of water, or on damp mud or leaves near the water surface. In some species the eggs hatch quickly and die if allowed to dry, but some species have eggs which are resistant to drying for long periods – up to several months. This is the reason that pots and other containers are sometimes seen to contain mosquito larvae only an hour or two after being filled with rain water, having been dry for a long time. The larvae are aquatic and swim with a wriggling motion. They come to the surface periodically to obtain air, when they hang from the surface film by the 'siphon' at the end of the body. The pupa is free-swimming and spends much of its time hanging from the surface. When the adult hatches, emergence from the pupa is very rapid and it is only a minute or so before the adult mosquito is able to fly away.

The main types of disease-carrying mosquitoes are *Aedes* (Plate 21), often black with silvery markings, which transmit virus diseases such as yellow fever and dengue fever; *Anopheles* (slender brown species) which transmit malaria; and *Culex* (usually dull brown) which transmit filariasis. Among the other West African mosquitoes are a couple which deserve special mention. *Toxorhynchites* are very large mosquitoes, the largest which occur in West Africa. They are about 2 cm long and very striking in appearance as they are covered in metallic blue, purple and orange-red scales. Despite their fierce appearance they are quite harmless as they have no biting mouthparts (in all mosquitoes it is only the females which bite, the males suck nectar or water). They have been used as a means of controlling other mosquitoes as the larvae are cannibalistic and feed on other mosquito larvae. *Toxorhynchites* larvae are often found in clean water in discarded pots and they are easily recognised by their large size and deep red colour. One large *Toxorhynchites* larva may kill up to twenty other mosquito larvae per day. They are not the only predaceous mosquito larvae as certain *Aedes* and the common *Culex tigripes* have the same habits.

The brown and white mottled *Mansonia* is very common over most of West Africa and is usually found plentifully near rivers or borrow-pits, where the water lettuce, *Pistia*, grows, although it may be found biting in large numbers some distance from water. The larva is interesting in that it has a specially modified siphon which it thrusts into the oxygen-containing tissues of water plants. It obtains its oxygen for breathing in this way and does not need to come to the surface to breathe. *Mansonia* mosquitoes also transmit virus diseases to man.

Gall midges (family Cecidomyiidae) are very small, often bright-orange or red flies with a wing length of only 2—3 mm. The larvae of some species feed on plant leaves, buds, flowers and stems, often deforming them and forming galls. Some species are important pests of crops. Black-flies (family Simuliidae) transmit a filarial worm which causes river blindness, a disease which is responsible for much misery in parts of West Africa. The adult flies are black with a somewhat humped appearance and are about 3—5 mm long. The larvae live in fast-flowing streams and rivers, attached to stones or water plants; in East Africa the larva of one species attaches itself to the backs of fresh-water crabs. The fly may be controlled by dosing streams and rivers with insecticide, but this has to be done with great care and under strict controls to prevent adverse effects on other water creatures and on people who may use the water further downstream.

Sandflies (family Phlebotomidae) are small flies only 2—3 mm long, with long legs and hairy wings which they carry above their backs when at rest. They are important as vectors of leishmaniasis (kala-azar) and sandfly fever in some parts of Africa, but those species found in West Africa do not seem to be important in the spread of disease. Indeed many of the species found feed upon reptiles but not on man. Non-biting midges (family Chironomidae) are found near water and their larvae are aquatic. They may occasionally occur in vast swarms and then become a considerable nuisance. One species, which lives in temporary rock-pools which are liable to dry out, has become adapted to this habitat and is able to survive desiccation. When dry it is very resistant to extremes of temperature — it can be placed in boiling water or cooled in liquid air and will still partially recover when placed in water at normal temperature. Biting midges (family Ceratopogonidae), although very tiny, being only about 1—2 mm long, bite fiercely and can make life outside unbearable in some areas. Some species are important because they transmit diseases to domestic livestock and birds, but other members of the same family are very beneficial to man in that they are responsible for the pollination of cocoa.

The second sub-order includes the horse-flies (family Tabanidae) which are well known for their painful bites. *Chrysops*, an orange and black fly, transmits the human filarial worm loa loa. Horse-flies are attracted by the shape and movement of a potential host, and will often land on or enter a slowly-driven car, mistaking it for a large animal. If you swat a horse-fly, take a look at its eyes before you discard it, as most species have beautiful patterns of iridescent spots and bands. Robber-flies (family Asilidae) are common and are often mistaken for biting flies since they have a horny proboscis extending from below the head. They are, however, quite harmless to humans and feed on other insects which they catch in flight. Flies of the family Empididae are found commonly near water. They have a horny proboscis and catch other insects in the same fashion as robber-flies. They have interesting mating habits in that the male captures a fly and presents it to the female who feeds upon it during mating. Bee-flies (family Bombyliidae) are often to be seen on flowers, they have very hairy bodies and patterned wings, and a long proboscis which they use for sucking nectar (Plate 22). The larvae are parasitic on the larvae of solitary bees and wasps, some attack grasshoppers and caterpillars, and others are parasites of tsetse flies.

The third sub-order contains a large assortment of families of very diverse form and habit. Hover-flies (family Syrphidae) often resemble bees and wasps and are frequently found on flowers. They are very accomplished fliers and are able to hover in one spot, hence the name. Flies of the family Diopsidae (Fig 33) are some of the most bizarre of all flies. They are found commonly in marshy places and along the banks of

eggs while others give birth to living larvae. Some have the unpleasant habit of infesting wounds in injured animals, sometimes causing death. Tumbu flies (Fig 34) are common pests in some areas, which lay their eggs on clothing or on the soil and the larvae burrow into the

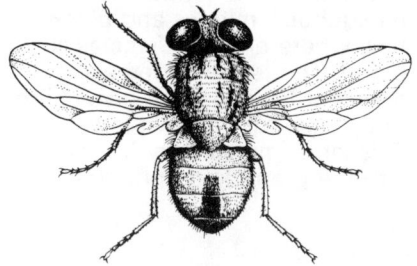

Fig 34   Adult tumbu fly, family Calliphoridae (Diptera)

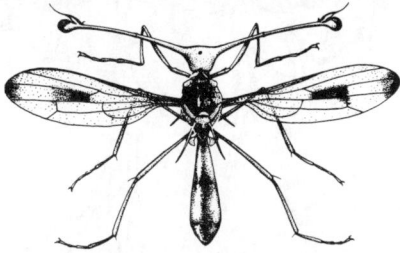

Fig 33   Member of the family Diopsidae (Diptera) — the eyes are rigid stalks on either side of the head

streams, usually sitting on twigs or grass stems. They are easily recognised as the eyes are borne on long rigid stalks from each side of the head. The ommatidia of each compound eye are arranged around the end of each stalk so that the insect must have a very wide field of vision. In some parts of West Africa diopsids are pests of rice, the larvae boring down inside the leaf sheath and feeding from the developing shoot.

Blow-flies (family Calliphoridae), despite their unpleasant habits, perform a valuable service since their maggots dispose of the corpses of animals. Some species lay

skin of man or animals. Puppies are often infested. The larva remains in the skin, causing a painful swelling, until fully grown when they drop out onto the ground and pupate. Tachinid flies (family Tachinidae) generally look like large, bristly house-flies and their larvae are parasitic in the bodies of the larvae of butterflies and moths, beetles, bugs and grasshoppers. The larvae feed upon the internal organs of their host, eventually killing it before emerging to pupate.

House-flies (family Muscidae) are too well-known a pest to need more than a passing mention. Closely related to them are the stable-flies, which bite cattle, horses and man. Other species of Muscidae (*Atherigona*) are important pests of sorghum as the maggots feed inside the developing shoots. Fourteen species of tsetse flies (family Glossinidae) occur in West Africa (Plate 23). They are of particular importance for their role in the transmission of sleeping sickness in man and animals. Both the males and the females bite, in contrast to mosquitoes, midges and blackflies where only the females suck blood. The tsetse fly female does not lay eggs, but gives birth to a single fully-grown larva. This larva immediately burrows into the ground and pupates.

Siphonaptera *(Fleas)*

These somewhat unpleasant insects are ectoparasites on mammals and birds. They are small brownish creatures (Fig 35) which are flattened laterally and this enables them to crawl easily through the hairs or

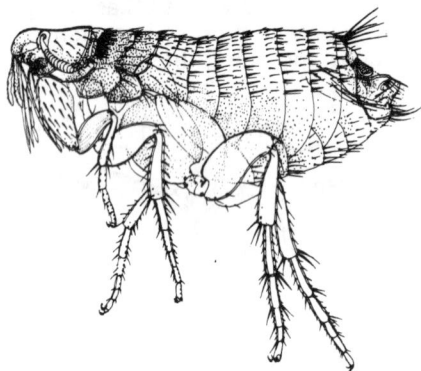

Fig 35   Adult flea (Siphonaptera)

feathers of their hosts. The adults have piercing and sucking mouthparts, and feed on blood. The hind legs are very powerful and are capable of propelling the flea in jumps of many times its own height and length. It is said, for instance, that the human flea can jump to a height of 20 cm and can leap horizontally a distance of well over 30 cm. None of the species of fleas have wings.

The eggs are dropped onto litter on floors or on the ground. The larvae are whitish with sparse long hairs and hide away in dust and dirt, feeding on any kind of organic debris. When mature, it spins a cocoon in which it pupates. Adult fleas can remain within their cocoon for many months without emerging, until stimulated to do so by the presence of a potential host. This is often seen in the case of dog fleas (*Ctenocephalides*), where a house which has been empty for some time suddenly appears infested with fleas as soon as someone enters. This is because the flea adults have been waiting in their cocoons in cracks and crevices, and between floor boards, and the vibrations caused by someone walking over the floor has stimulated the fleas to emerge.

Most fleas are host-specific, that is they prefer to bite one particular species of bird or animal, but when hungry they will attempt to bite any potential host. Anyone who has kept a dog or cat which has fleas will have noticed that they themselves seldom get bitten while the animal is around, but if for any reason the animal is removed, humans will be attacked.

Fleas are not only of importance for the annoyance caused by their bites but they are also of great medical importance as disease transmitters. The most notorious of the fleas is the rat flea (*Xenopsylla*) which transmits the bacilli which cause plague. Plague is primarily a disease of rodents, particularly of rats; the danger to humans arises when a rat suffering from the disease dies since the fleas will then leave the body and if hungry fleas happen to bite a human being, the disease will be transmitted. They are also responsible for the transmission of murine typhus, and several other unpleasant diseases. Fleas are

the intermediate hosts of tapeworms of dogs and cats because the flea larvae swallow the tapeworm eggs while feeding. The tapeworm then develops within the body of the flea, and the host animal becomes infected when an infected flea is eaten.

Another unpleasant type of flea is the 'jigger' (*Tunga penetrans*). Man and pigs are usually attacked but cats and dogs may also be infested. The male of these fleas bites in the usual manner, but the female burrows into the skin of the host. There she swells up enormously as the eggs develop within her abdomen. The site usually chosen is the heel, the big toe, under a toe nail or between the toes and the fleas are often picked up by walking barefoot. The swellings caused give rise to intense soreness and irritation.

Hymenoptera
(Ants, Wasps and Bees)

This is a very large order of insects, with many species which are directly or indirectly beneficial to man. Their behaviour is interesting because of the various degrees of social organisation they exhibit, from solitary insects to the truly social bees and wasps which live in highly organised colonies with many thousands of individuals.

Most species have two pairs of clear, membranous wings. In the majority the female has an ovipositor which is used for piercing animal or plant tissues and some species are capable of giving a nasty sting with it or a bite with their well-developed, powerful jaws. They are usually well-built insects with a very hard thorax. There may be a well-defined 'waist' between the thorax and abdomen. The typical life-cycle is of the egg — larva — pupa — adult type; the larvae are usually white legless 'grubs' but the larvae of sawflies look very like the caterpillars of moths.

Sawflies are among the most primitive members of the order, and belong to a group of families which lack the distinct 'waist' between the thorax and the abdomen. The adults are frequently found on flowers. The ovipositor is modified for piercing plant tissues, in which the eggs are laid, but although they look fierce they do not sting. The larvae feed on the leaves of plants, bushes and trees; they are often greenish in colour with black spots and have a dark distinct head. They resemble moth larvae but may be distinguished from them by having a greater number of legs. Sawflies can cause considerable damage to crops by boring into stems or by defoliating plants.

Ichneumon-flies (family Ichneumonidae) have a very long ovipositor and long, thin antennae. They seek out other insects, particularly caterpillars. The female lays one or more eggs in the body of the caterpillar and when the grub hatches it devours the internal organs of its host. When fully grown, the grub emerges and pupates in a silken cocoon, often spun on the now shrivelled body of its host. Some ichneumons prey on the larvae of wood-boring beetles and moths, and can detect the larvae through a considerable thickness of wood. In these cases the ovipositor is used to bore through the solid wood to reach the host within, and it is one of the marvels of the insect world how they are able to locate the host so precisely and to place an egg accurately within its body. Ichneumon-flies are very beneficial to man, for the role they play in controlling the numbers of insects which are injurious to crops. Wasps of a closely related family, the Braconidae, are also insect parasites and thus equally beneficial, but here large numbers of wasp grubs are often found within a single host. Some tiny braconids are parasites of aphids. Wasps of the family Evaniidae (Fig 36) are tiny blackish insects with the abdomen compressed laterally and held up on a long

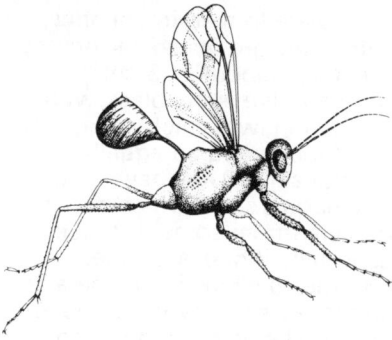

Fig 36   Ensign fly, family
          Evaniidae (Hymenoptera)

stalk like a small flag. They are
parasites within the oothecae of
cockroaches. The wasp lays a
single egg in each ootheca and
when the wasp grub hatches,
it eats all of the cockroach eggs
before it matures.

Fig trees are numerous in West
Africa although the fruits are
inedible, but they would
disappear if it were not for the
activities of the fig-wasps (family
Agaontidae). The eggs are laid
within the developing figs, in
which the larvae develop and
mature. When the adults emerge
they mate within the figs. Only
the female wasps can fly and
when they eventually escape
from the fig they become dusted
with pollen. They fly off and
enter young figs on the same or
on different trees, at the right
stage of development, where
they lay their eggs and
incidentally fertilise the fig with
the pollen they are carrying.
Although the wasps can enter
the developing fig, they are
unable to escape from it and

having laid their eggs, they die.
It has been found that each
species of fig has its own
characteristic species of fig-wasp.
These wasps are of great
economic importance where figs
are grown as a commercial crop.

Allied to the fig-wasps are a
number of families of minute
insects, collectively known as
chalcid wasps. These parasitise a
wide range of hosts, including
flies, ants, aphids and caterpillars.
Some are so tiny that they are
able to develop within the eggs
of butterflies and moths. The
details of their biology are a
fascinating study in themselves.

Cuckoo-wasps (family
Chrysididae) are stoutly built
wasps about 1 cm long or less.
They are a brilliant metallic blue
or green in colour and some, the
'ruby-tail wasps', have the
abdomen coloured a brilliant
metallic red. The adults lay their
eggs in the nests of solitary
bees and wasps, within which
they develop.

Ants are a familiar sight in the
tropics, and here again there is an
enormous diversity of form and
habits within the group. They
are all classified into one large
family, the Formicidae, but this
is divided into several subfamilies.
Most ants live in highly organised
colonies which may have a few
to many thousands of individuals.
Normally a colony contains three
types or castes of ants: a queen,
the males, and workers. Unlike
the termite colonies there is no
'king' or functional male and the
male dies after a short mating
flight. At certain times large
numbers of winged males and
females are produced, and when

conditions are favourable these leave the nest on their brief mating flight. As in the termites, this mass exodus is usually synchronised over a wide area so that interbreeding of the colonies is ensured.

Ants, principally *Camponotus* and *Pheidole*, have recently been shown to be involved in the spread of pod rot, a fungus disease of cocoa. *Pheidole* ants also tend the mealybugs which are the vectors of cocoa swollen shoot disease virus. Ants tending bugs on cocoa trees carry soil up the trees to make tents or shelters over the bugs and if this soil is infected with fungus then infection of the cocoa pods can result. It has recently been found that the balance between colonies of various species of ants is of great importance in cocoa plantations. These inter-relationships are very complex and are the subject of much research. Studies of ant populations on cocoa in Ghana and Nigeria have shown that there is a very delicate balance between the different species of ants and particularly between weaver ants and other species. These studies are of great importance in our understanding of how diseases of cocoa may be controlled.

One of the most primitive of the subfamilies is the Ponerinae, familiar in West Africa as the 'stink ants'. They differ from other ants in that their nests consist of relatively few individuals, usually only a dozen or so. The workers, queens and males are about the same size and the pupae are formed in cocoons. Stink ants are fearsome-looking creatures, about 2–3 cm long and are shiny black with powerful jaws which can give a painful bite and an equally painful sting. They have a very unpleasant smell which can be detected from some distance, especially if one is crushed. I find the smell distinctly metallic, rather like some types of metal polish. The nest is a deep hole in the ground, without a mound of earth to mark its location. The principal prey of the ants is said to be termites and their larvae are fed on pieces of insects which have been captured.

The subfamily Dorylinae includes the soldier or driver ants (Plate 24). No one who has seen these insects on the move could mistake them. They travel in dense columns of marching ants and these columns, which may be 5 cm or more across, have been recorded as taking a day or more to pass. The workers are blind, with large powerful jaws. The queen is very seldom seen but is three or four times the size of a worker and is also blind. In addition to the workers there is a 'soldier' caste with very large toothed jaws, and there are many intermediate forms between workers and soldiers. They all have a very powerful bite and once their jaws are fixed in position it is very difficult to make them let go. If they are pulled off, the head and jaws are often left attached to the unfortunate victim. The nest is formed in a hollow in the earth, often under a log or in an old termite mound and colonies can contain hundreds of thousands of individuals.

Periodic forays are made from the nest when the ants hunt over a wide area, killing for food any living creature in their path which is not fast enough to escape. There is even a record of an African python, which having just fed was too sluggish to move, being killed and devoured. These ants often kill poultry and if they invade a house they will completely clear it of vermin. Driver ants are usually carnivorous but vegetable food and fruits are occasionally eaten. Every few weeks the whole colony moves house and they progress in a long column; eggs, larvae, pupae and even food is carried by the workers and the column is flanked by soldiers which keep guard. The queen is also said to be carried by the workers, but how this is done seems not to have been observed, so here is an area where patient (and cautious!) observation would add to our knowledge. Despite the abundance of driver ants, little is known of their habits or of the factors which cause their mass migrations, although work in Central America has suggested that this may be related to the egg-laying cycles of the queen. Although queen driver ants are rarely seen, the male driver ants are the familiar 'sausage-flies' (Fig 37) which are often attracted to lights. They are about 2.5 cm long, brown and with a stout cylindrical body. They do not sting.

Ants belonging to the subfamily Myrmicinae make their nests on the trunks or on the larger branches of trees. The nests look as though they are made of black earth, but in reality are made of a tough, papery material. Ants of this subfamily often have complex associations with the larvae of 'blue' butterflies of the family Lycaenidae which feed on lichens growing on tree trunks. The larvae derive protection from the presence of the ants, which are in turn rewarded by the production of a sticky, sugary secretion from special glands on the body of the larva. This association between ants and other insects is not confined to butterflies since it occurs with aphids, coccids and membracid bugs as mentioned in the sections dealing with those insects. In East Africa the coffee mealybug was a great pest, being attended by ants which not only protected the bugs but actually seemed to stimulate the growth of colonies of bugs by their presence. For many years the only practical form of control was to put grease-bands on the tree trunks

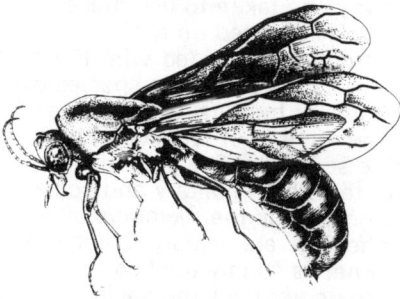

Fig 37   Male driver ant or 'sausage fly', subfamily Dorylinae (Hymenoptera)

to prevent ants from reaching the bugs. The picture was further complicated by the discovery that in some cases populations of weaver ants helped to reduce bug populations because of their aggressive behaviour towards the ants tending the bugs. Much the same mechanisms seem to operate among the ants in cocoa plantations as mentioned above.

Some insects spend part or all of their life in the nests of ants (and also in the nests of wasps and bees), either living off ant larvae or by acting as scavengers within the nest. Examples of insects which live in ants' nests and feed on ant larvae are the lycaenid butterflies *Lachnocnema* (the larvae are found in ants' nests below ground) and *Euliphyra* (the larvae are found in the nests of weaver ants on trees).

The weaver or tailor ants (*Oecophylla*) have already been mentioned, and in some ways these are the most remarkable of all ants. They belong to the subfamily Formicinae and the workers are about 1 cm long, pale brown and with a pair of powerful jaws. The queen is much larger and pale brownish in colour. The nest is formed in trees and bushes and is made up of bunches of leaves drawn together with silk (Plate 25). In making the nest, groups of workers pull two leaves together with their jaws and other workers bind them with silk produced by the weaver ant larvae which they hold in their jaws, waving them back and forth until the leaves are securely held. This is often quoted as the only known example of an insect using a tool. I have not seen an account of how a nest is started by a queen, but presumably she lays a small batch of eggs perhaps in a shelter abandoned by some other insect, and when the first brood matures nest construction begins properly.

There are many other types of ant; the familiar 'sugar ant' or Pharaoh's ant (*Monomorium pharaonis*) is one example. These tiny ants are found in houses wherever there is food. They have the uncanny ability to find their way into food containers even when they appear to be tightly sealed, and are extremely hard to eradicate. Probably the best method to destroy ants is to use one of the proprietary poison baits designed for ants. These contain an attractive sugary substance and a stomach poison which is ingested and then taken back to the nest. Since ants often feed their larvae and other workers with regurgitated food in the nest, the poison is spread to other individuals and the nest is soon decimated. Great care should always be taken to use these baits as directed on the instructions provided with them.

There are two main species of wasps, or hornets, each with a large number of families of diverse habits. The Vespidae contains both solitary and social insects while the members of the Sphecidae are solitary. The name 'hornet' is strictly applied to *Vespa crabro*, a large social yellow and brown insect found in temperate climates, but the term is often applied to any large, fearsome-looking vespid wasp.

The nests of 'hornets' are a familiar sight (Plate 26). They are found attached to walls, ceilings, branches or any other convenient support in a sheltered site and consist of a few papery cells (usually up to a dozen) attached by a thin stalk with the open ends of the cells downwards. The first cells are made by a single female, although sometimes more than one will make a communal nest. There are usually a few hornets in attendance, sitting on the cells of the nest. They are fierce-looking insects, often very large, 3–4 cm long, with sleek streamlined bodies and often black or metallic blue in colour. There are no sterile workers, the males stay by the nest and the females hunt the prey which often consists of caterpillars. Eggs are laid in the cells which are left open and the larvae anchor themselves in the cell by hooks at the hind end of the body. Chewed and partially digested insect prey is fed to the larvae when the females return to the nest. All hornets can give a painful sting and should not be handled.

An example of the family Sphecidae is the mud-dauber wasp, a large yellow and black species, some 3–4 cm long, which makes the mud cells often found in houses, usually in some inaccessible corner (Fig 38). Up to a dozen cells may be made in a group. The female wasp collects mud in her jaws and forms it into a cylindrical cell about 1 cm wide by 3 cm long and open at one end. When the cell is complete she flies off to hunt

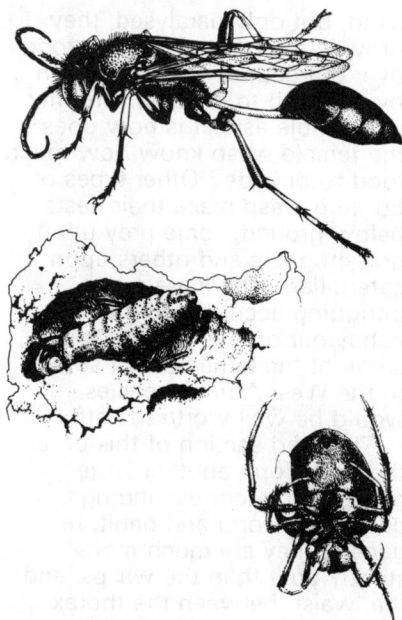

Fig 38   Mud-dauber wasp, family Sphecidae (Hymenoptera) – an egg attached to a paralysed spider and a fully-grown larva in its cell cell of dried mud

for spiders. These are stung by the wasp with great precision, so that they become paralysed but do not die. They are then taken back to the cell and stuffed inside. When sufficient have been collected the wasp lays an egg on one of the spiders and seals the cell with mud. When the wasp grub hatches it feeds on the spiders and just sufficient food is provided to allow the grub to develop to maturity. It then pupates within the cell and eventually emerges as an adult wasp. The remarkable thing is that since the spiders are not dead, but only paralysed, they provide the grub with fresh food over the couple of weeks taken by the grub to develop. Another remarkable aspect is how does the female wasp know how much food to provide? Other types of hunting wasp make their nests below ground; some prey upon grasshoppers and others upon caterpillars. There are many intriguing accounts of the behaviour of these wasps, and a study of the behaviour of some of the West African species would be well worth the effort.

The third section of this order, the bees, form another large group with a corresponding diversity in form and habit. In general they are much more stoutly built than the wasps, and the 'waist' between the thorax and abdomen is not conspicuous, although present. They also differ from wasps in that they feed on nectar and pollen, and do not hunt other insects.

Leaf-cutting bees (family Megachilidae) cut circular or oval holes in the leaves of plants, and use the pieces to form cells, usually in a hollow twig. These cells are packed with a mixture of pollen and honey and a single egg is laid in each cell. Up to a dozen cells may be formed, built end to end. Leaf-cutting bees are sometimes a source of annoyance to gardeners for the damage they may do to plants, such as roses or cannas, but they are seldom a serious pest.

The family Apidae includes a large number of interesting insects, of which there is space here to mention only three: the carpenter-bees, the sweat-bees and the honey-bees. Carpenter-bees are conspicuous both for their large size (they are among the largest of the bees) and for their blackish-blue colour. The nests are often made in the dry dead branches of trees. They bore out a hole inside the wood in which they form chambers, laid end to end. These are provisioned with honey and pollen and an egg is laid in each. They are then sealed with a mixture of wood chips and saliva. The occupants of the inner cells, which are the oldest (the eggs having been laid first) are the last to emerge from the nest, since they have to make their way through the cells of the younger members of the brood to get to the outside world. When these bees are making their nest the sound of their boring can create an eerie effect, especially if they are boring into house timbers.

Sweat-bees, or wax-tunnel bees, are very tiny and only 3—4 mm long. They are very troublesome in some areas for their habit of settling on exposed skin to suck perspiration, but they have only a vestigial sting and are not aggressive, although they can bite if sufficiently provoked. They make their nests in cracks in walls, holes in trees and often around window frames. There is a short tunnel, about 2—3 cm long and made of wax, leading into the nest and this tunnel is closed at night. These are 'social' bees and live in colonies of several hundred individuals. The larvae are reared and tended by sterile female 'workers' within the nest. The honey produced by these bees is said to be strong and aromatic, but the nests are usually too inaccessible to make its gathering worthwhile.

An account of the biology of the honey-bee would occupy a whole book in itself. It is one of the most useful of all insects to man in its role of a pollinator of flowers and fruit, and for the honey which bee colonies provide. A colony consists of sterile female 'workers', males or 'drones' and one or more queens. There are very many races or varieties of the honey-bee, which is semi-domesticated in many parts of the world. In northern Nigeria they are kept in 'hives' of rolls of grass or rush matting wedged in the branches of trees, and the honey is much in demand. The African strain of the honey-bee has a reputation for its bad temper and many cases of death resulting from multiple stings have been recorded. Nests of honey-bees should be given a wide berth and should never be interferred with unless one is expert in handling bees. Worker bees communicate the distance and direction of a source of nectar to other members of the hive by performing a special kind of dance at the entrance to the hive. They are able to orient themselves by detecting the plane of polarisation of the light coming from the sky.

Coleoptera *(Beetles)*

The beetles form one of the largest orders of insects. It has been estimated that there may be about two hundred thousand species known in the world, and more are being described every year. With the destruction of habitats by man and in particular the destruction of vast areas of natural forest for the doubtful short-term advantages of commercial gain, many species are being lost before we have even had a chance to discover them!

Beetles include some of the smallest and the largest of the West African insects. Despite the enormous variety of form and colour, most are easy to recognise as beetles since the fore-wings are modified to form a pair of hard, horny wing-cases, the elytra. These protect the membranous hind-wings, which are folded under the elytra when not in use. When in flight, the elytra are raised above the back of the insect and are not moved. Some beetles have the elytra reduced so that they do not completely cover the abdomen and they might be mistaken for earwigs, but they have no pincers at the end of the body. A typical beetle has a life-history of egg – larva – pupa – adult although there are many variations on this basic theme and the life-histories of some beetles are quite remarkable. As might be expected in such a diverse order, there are a large number of families of beetles and only a few of the more interesting will be mentioned here.

Tiger-beetles (family Cicindelidae) may often be seen on sunny paths in forest or farmland by day. They fly for a short distance, then settle on the ground and run about rapidly. They are usually about 2 cm long, a deep metallic green or black colour and they have very large jaws and prominent eyes (Plate 27). The larva lives in a deep vertical burrow in the ground and lies in wait for any insect which passes near to the entrance. The larva then seizes it and the victim is dragged below ground and eaten.

The ground-beetles (Plate 28) which belong to the family Carabidae, are numerous everywhere. They are found under stones, logs, in rotting vegetation and are frequently attracted to light. In many species the elytra are fused together and the insects cannot fly but there are also species which live in trees and can fly freely. Most ground-beetles and their larvae feed on other insects and as they frequently destroy insect pests, they can be regarded as friends of man.

Wherever there is water there are beetles living either on the surface or below. There are a number of different families of these water-beetles. The Dytiscidae spend much of their time hunting below the surface, while in the Gyrinidae the adults dart to and fro on the surface. Water-beetles can breathe, when below the surface, by using a bubble of air trapped below the elytra, which is periodically renewed by visits to the surface. Some water-beetles have a thick layer of modified hairs on their backs which traps a film of air and enables the beetle to stay under water by allowing gaseous exchange with the oxygen dissolved in the water. Many beetles of this type cling to the surface of rocks in fast-flowing streams. The beetles cannot remain below the surface indefinitely, however, since the nitrogen in the air film gradually dissolves in the water and the beetle must eventually come to the surface to renew the air film. Water-beetles are carnivorous and feed on other insects and water creatures. They are good fliers.

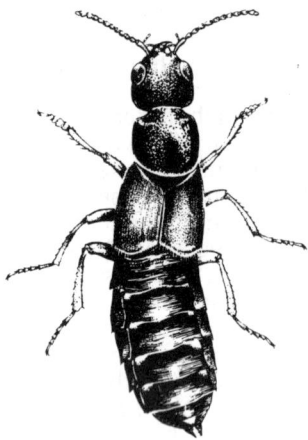

Fig 39   Rove-beetle, family Staphylinidae (Coleoptera)

Rove-beetles (family Staphylinidae) have very short elytra which only cover a small part of the abdomen (Fig 39). They are mostly small brownish beetles, 1 cm or less, although there are a few larger species. They may be found under stones, among rotting vegetation or decaying animal matter. There are some small, bright orange-coloured species with bluish-black elytra which can cause nasty blisters if they are crushed on the skin.

The family Scarabaeidae contains a range of beetles which will be familiar to most readers. Chafer-beetles are no friend of the gardener because of the activities of the adults, which feed on the leaves or flowers of plants. The larvae are whitish with large brown heads and long front legs and they curl up into a circle when disturbed. They feed on the roots of plants below ground and can cause consider-able damage when present in numbers. Dung-beetles (Plate 29) are for the most part black or dirty brown, and may be seen laboriously rolling a ball of dung along the ground. These balls are buried and eaten by the adults. The eggs are laid in larger balls of dung in which the larva lives, feeds and pupates. The beetles perform a valuable service by burying enormous quantities of animal dung.

Rhinoceros-beetles are easily recognised by the large, upturned 'horn' on the head of the male although in the female the horn is much smaller. They are large brown beetles which are a serious pest of oil palms and coconut palms. The larva is a fat white grub like the chafer larva. They often infest the growing shoots of palm trees and when they do so they may kill the tree by destroying the shoot. The larva takes about two to three months to mature and the adult

beetles may live for three to four months. The larvae also live in rotting palm trunks, and it is important to clear rotting trees from plantations to control infestations of the beetle. The rhinoceros-beetle is a good example of a successful attempt at biological control of an insect pest. In Mauritius it caused great damage but was controlled by the introduction of a parasitic wasp from the Malagasy Republic in 1917. Hercules-beetles (Fig 40) may be very large, up to 8 cm or so. They have a large horn on the thorax as well as one on the head.

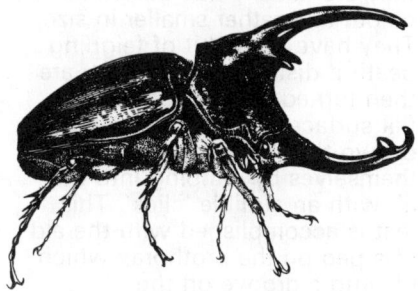

Fig 40   Hercules beetle, family
Scarabaeidae (Coleoptera)

Goliath-beetles (Plate 30) are the largest of the West African beetles — they may be up to 10 cm long by 5 cm broad. They are very distinctive apart from their size as they are a dark, velvety brown colour with prominent white lines on the thorax. Several species are found in forest regions but although widely distributed they are not often seen. Less spectacular but more important to the farmer is the yam-beetle. It is blackish and about 2 cm long. The adults can do enormous damage by burrowing into yam tubers and rendering them unfit for sale. The larvae feed on the roots of a variety of plants in swampy habitats.

The Buprestidae, which have no common name, may often be seen in forests where they fly freely, often during the day. They are mostly fairly large, measuring 2 cm or more, and are often brilliantly coloured with metallic green or blue (Plate 31). The larvae bore into wood. The click-beetles (family Elateridae) are similar to the buprestids in general appearance, although they are usually dull brown in colour and rather smaller in size. They have the habit of feigning death if disturbed but if they are then turned on their back on a flat surface and left for a minute or two they suddenly right themselves by jumping into the air with an audible 'click'. This feat is accomplished with the aid of a peg on the prothorax which fits into a groove on the mesothorax. When the thorax is flexed, the peg suddenly springs out of the groove and the sudden jerk propels the insect into the air. The larvae of click-beetles are commonly known as 'wireworms'. They feed below ground on the roots of plants and can cause considerable damage to crops.

One of the most remarkable of the beetles is the glow-worm (family Lampyridae), more often recognised after dark by its flashing light than by its appearance by day. They are small beetles, only about 1 cm long, and dull brown in colour (Fig 41). In some species the

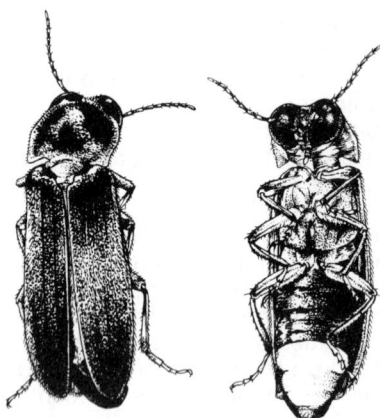

Fig 41   Glow-worm beetles or fire-flies, family Lampyridae (Coleoptera) — dorsal and ventral views to show the light-producing area at the tip of the abdomen

males only are winged but in others both sexes can fly. The light which they produce is emitted from special areas under the abdomen and is produced chemically by the action of an enzyme called 'luciferase' upon a substance called 'luciferin'. This process of light production is highly efficient as very little (only about 2%) of the energy is lost in heat. The larvae are carnivorous and feed upon snails and slugs. A few other insects are able to emit light: some Collembola, some Hemiptera (lantern-flies) and some beetles of the family Elateridae.

The Dermestidae (hide-beetles or carpet-beetles) is another family of small beetles. They are mostly less than 1 cm long, blackish and covered with fine hair. The larvae are very destructive pests of stored products, especially hides and skins. In West Africa dermestids are particularly important pests of dried meat and dried fish. Wood-boring beetles belong to a number of families; they are small brownish insects which can do serious damage to the timbers of buildings and to furniture. A number of other families contain members that are serious pests of stored products. It has been estimated that between 5 and 10% of the world's grain harvest is lost through the activities of insect pests. Man must wage a constant campaign against them to keep them under control.

Ladybird beetles (family Coccinellidae) have a characteristic rounded shape. They are usually small but brightly coloured red or yellow with black spots, or sometimes black with red or yellow spots. Both the adults and the larvae are carnivorous and feed principally upon aphids and other small bugs. For this reason they are very beneficial to man.

Blister-beetles and oil-beetles (family Meloidae) contain a substance which causes severe blistering if rubbed on the skin. They have a particularly interesting life-history. The eggs of oil-beetles are laid on the ground and the tiny larvae which hatch from them are very active. They climb onto vegetation or flowers. If a larva is lucky enough to encounter a solitary bee it attaches itself to the bee's body and is carried back to the

bee's nest, where it feeds upon the eggs and larvae of its host. Blister-beetles (Plate 32) have a similar life-history but feed on the egg-pods of grasshoppers. The eggs of these beetles are laid in very large numbers, as might be expected, for very many tiny larvae die before they can locate a suitable host.

The reason that longhorn beetles (family Cerambycidae) are so called is immediately obvious – the antennae are greatly elongated and the span of these could qualify them for the title of the largest known insects (Plate 33). One specimen of a brown and black longhorn which was given to me in Lagos had a body of 5–6 cm long, but the antennae spanned 37 cm. Many long-horns are attractively coloured being yellow, red or green; some are perfectly camouflaged to resemble the bark of trees; while others are brown or black. The larvae bore into the stems of plants or bushes, or into the wood of trees. The life-cycle of these wood-boring species is often long, sometimes more than a year. When they occur in large numbers they can cause considerable damage to timber and some species are pests of coffee and cocoa.

Weevils (family Curculionidae) are again distinctive since the head is drawn out into a long 'snout' (Fig 42). Most weevils are small and dull-coloured, and many are important pests of crops and stored products. The larva of the maize weevil bores into the grains to feed and it is often not until the cobs have been

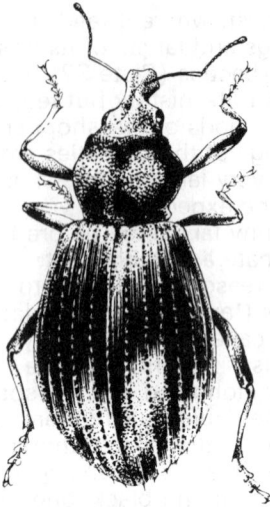

Fig 42   Weevil, family
          Curculionidae (Coleoptera) —
          the snout may be short or very
          long

only problem for the aspiring
entomologist is the identification
of his captures and the best
course would be to seek the
advice of an entomologist at the
nearest university.

stored that the damage caused by
the feeding of the larva becomes
apparent. Cowpeas, rice and
garri are also all liable to attack
by weevils and infestations are
a cause of serious annual loss to
farmers, traders and consumers
alike.

As stated earlier, it has only
been possible to mention a few of
the families of beetles. There is
much to be said for further and
more detailed study of this order
in West Africa. As has been seen,
many are of direct importance to
man; the habits of only a few
have been investigated in detail
and many more species remain
to be described. They preserve
well in a collection, their
colours do not easily fade and a
large number of species can be
found within a small area. The

Strepsiptera *(Stylops)*

These tiny insects are only rarely seen or recognised, although they are not in fact uncommon. They are usually classified by entomologists as being related to the beetles. The males have a single pair of wings while the females are wingless. In the Diptera, which also have one pair of wings, the hind-pair has been reduced and modified, but in the stylops it is the fore-wings which have been reduced and are represented by small club-like structures. The wings of the males are broad, fan-shaped and membranous and they have curious branched antennae. They are sometimes attracted to light but are seldom noticed, being less than 0.5 cm across the wings. The females are degenerate maggot-like creatures without legs or even a well-defined head.

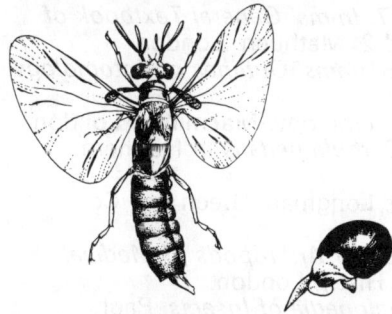

Fig 43   Male (winged) and female stylops (Strepsiptera)

Stylops (Fig 43) are internal parasites of solitary bees, wasps and bugs (for example the leaf-hopper bugs which infest rice). Their life-cycle is remarkable. The eggs are laid on plants, being dropped there when a parasitised insect visits a flower. These hatch into minute but very active larvae which crawl about on the flowers. If they are lucky enough to encounter an insect of the right species to act as host they attach themselves and burrow into the body of the host. Here they moult into small maggot-like creatures devoid of limbs and mouthparts and they feed by absorbing nourishment from the blood of the host through the larval skin. Eventually its metamorphosis is completed but without killing the host. The males emerge and fly away but the female remains within the body of the host with only the head end protruding from between two segments of the host's body. The physiological disturbances caused by the presence of the stylops usually renders the host sterile and some changes may be found in the external characters of a parasitised host, for example changes in colour patterns. Stylops are not of any economic importance to man, as they do not occur in large enough numbers to affect populations of their insect hosts.

References

Andrewes, Sir C. 1969. *The Lives of Wasps and Bees*. Chatto and Windus, London.

Anon. 1966. *The Locust Handbook*. The Anti-Locust Research Centre, London.

Boorman, J. 1970. *West African Butterflies and Moths*. West African Nature Handbooks. Longman, London.

Busvine, J.R. 1966. *Insects and Hygiene*. 2nd edn. Methuen, London.

Caswell, G.H. 1962. *Agricultural Entomology in the Tropics*. Edward Arnold, London.

Ene, J.C. 1963. *Insects and Man in West Africa*. Ibadan University Press.

Ezueh, M. 1978. *Introduction to Economic Entomology*. Ethiope Publishing Corp.

Kirkpatrick, T.W. 1957. *Insect Life in the Tropics*. Longman, Green and Co., London.

Klots, A.B. and Klots, E.B. 1959. *Living Insects of the World*. Hamish Hamilton, London.

Kranz, J., Schmutterer, H. and Kock, W. 1977. *Diseases, Pests and Weeds in Tropical Crops*. John Wiley and Sons, Chichester.

Malaka, S.L. Omo. 1973. Observations on Termites in Nigeria. *Nigerian Field* 38: 24–40.

Medler, J.T. 1979. Insects of Nigeria – Check List and Bibliography. *Mem. Am. Ent. Inst.* No. 30

Pinhey, E.C.G. 1973. *Introduction to Insect Study in Africa*. Oxford University Press, London.

Richards, O.W. and Davies, R.G. 1977. *Imms' General Textbook of Entomology*. 10th edn., vols 1 and 2. Methuen, London.

Richards, O.W. and Davies R.G. 1978. *Imms' Outlines of Entomology*. 6th edn. Methuen, London.

Romoser, A. 1973. *The Science of Entomology*. Macmillan, London.

Service, M.W. 1963. Infestations of *Carbula pedalis* in Northern Nigeria. *Nature* 194: 213–214.

Skaife, S.H. 1954. *African Insect Life*. Longman, Green and Co., London.

Smith, K.G.V. ed. 1973. *Insects and Other Arthropods of Medical Importance*. British Museum (Nat. Hist.), London.

Stanek, V.J. 1969. *The Pictorial Encyclopedia of Insects*. Paul Hamlyn, London.

Taylor, W.E. 1969. *Agricultural Pest Handbook*. Njola University College.

Thistleton, G.F. 1966. *Insects*. Nature Study for Africa Series. Evans Bros., London.

Tweedie, M. 1977. *Insect Life*. Collins Countryside Series. Collins, London.

Youdeowei, A. 1974. *The dissection of the variegated grasshopper, Zonocerus variegatus*. Oxford University Press, London.

Youdeowei, A. 1975. *Our Common Insects*. Ibadan University Press.
Youdeowei, A. 1977. *A Laboratory Manual of Entomology*. Oxford University Press, London.
Youdeowei, A. 1978. Macmillan Basic Science Readers. Book 3, *Insects*; Book 4, *Relatives of Insects*. Macmillan, London.

Index

References to plates are in bold.

of coconut palm 77
of coffee 51, 79
of cotton 49, 52
of cowpea 52, 54, 59, 80
of dried meat and fish 79
of garri 80
of kapok 52
of maize 17, 44, 59
of oil palm 77
of rice 48, 65, 80
of sorghum 65
of stored products 79
of sugar 51
of yams 44, 77
pharaoh's ant 72
phase, solitary and gregarious 18
Phasmida 19, **9**
Pheidole 70
Pheromone 1, 7
Phlebotomidae 64
Phyllocrania **10**
Pistia 63
plague 67
Plecoptera 15
poison bait 6, 72
Polistes **26**
pollination 6, 64
pollution 12, 14
pond skater 51
preservatives 8
prothorax 2
Protura 10
Psocid, Psocoptera 44
Pthirus 46
pupa 4
Pyrrhocoridae 52, **16**

queen ant 69
    termite 41

rat flea 67
red locust 18
Reduviidae 51, **14**
relapsing fever 46
rhinoceros beetle 77
Rickettsia 46
river blindness 6, 63
robber-fly 64
rove beetle 76

Sahlbergella 52, **15**
sandfly, sandfly fever 64
Saturniidae 59
sausage fly 71

sawfly 68
scale-insects 50, **13**
Scarabaeidae 77, **29**, **30**
scavengers 6
Schistocerca gregaria 18
scientific name 4
scorpion 1
scorpion-fly 58, **7**
screw-worm fly 8
Selenothrips 55
shield bug 53, **17**
short-horned grasshopper 16
silk, silkworm 59
silverfish 10
Simuliidae 63
Siphonaptera 66
Siphunculata 45
sleeping sickness 6, 62
social bees 74
social organisation 5
soldier ants 70
    termites 41, 43
species 4
Sphecidae 72, 73
Sphodromantis 23
spiders 1
spirochaete 46
sprays 7
springtails 10
stable-fly 65
Staphylinidae 76
sterile males 8
stick-insects 19, **9**
stoneflies 15
Strepsiptera 81
stridulation 16
Stylops 81
sub-imago 11, 12
sugar ant 72
swallow-tail 59
sweat-bee 74
Syntomidae 24
Syrphidae 65

Tabanidae 64
Tachinidae 65
Taeniothrips 55
tailor ant 72
tape-worm 67
tarsus 3
termites 41, **11**
Tettigoniidae 16, **3**
Thaumetopoeidae 59
thorax 2